A

SHARE~A~BOOK CLUB

DONATED BY

Gloria Shimkovitz

IN MEMORY OF

Rachel Blegen

J. D. BANCROFT ~ 1994

PRACTICAL GARDENING LIBRARY

THE WEEKEND
GARDENER

PRACTICAL GARDENING LIBRARY

THE WEEKEND
GARDENER

PETER McHOY
Photography by John Freeman

LORENZ BOOKS

This edition published by Lorenz Books
an imprint of
Anness Publishing Limited
Hermes House
88-89 Blackfriars Road
London SE1 8HA

Published in the USA by Lorenz Books
Anness Publishing Inc., 27 West 20th Street, New York, NY 10011;
(800) 354-9657

A CIP catalogue record for this book is available from the British Library

ISBN 0 7548 0040 7

Publisher: Joanna Lorenz
Senior Editor: Lindsay Porter
Designer: David Stanley
Photographer: John Freeman

Also published as part of the Step By Step Series

Printed and bound in China

© Anness Publishing Limited 1998
Updated © 1999

3 5 7 9 10 8 6 4

CONTENTS

Introduction	**6**
What is Low-Maintenance Gardening?	**8**
THE GARDEN FLOOR	**16**
BEDS AND BORDERS	**30**
EASY-CARE CONTAINERS	**64**
SMART IDEAS	**72**
WEEDING AND FEEDING	**82**
Index of Common Plant Names	**94**
Index	**95**

INTRODUCTION

Gardens should always be objects of beauty and give an immense sense of satisfaction, but they can also be demanding, and there is often a fine line between one that is a source of pleasure and one that becomes a worry or even a burden. For garden-lovers, lack of enthusiasm is rarely the problem; it is usually lack of time. This book is about making sure you have all the pleasures that a garden can bring, with few of the drawbacks.

There is nothing second-rate about a low-maintenance garden. It does not even necessarily mean cutting down on the number of plants that you grow. The choice of plants, and how you use them, is important. A low-maintenance garden can be every bit as interesting and attractive as one that is demanding in upkeep.

If hard surfaces and strong lines are more important to you than the number or range of plants, there is much scope for imaginative design that will have plenty of punch and impact with a minimal number of plants.

Even if you have never gardened before, you can probably transform your garden more easily than you realize, and this book will take you through all that you need to know for an attractive but minimum-effort garden, step-by-step.

If you are already an experienced gardener, and understand the principles of planting and cultivation, you will still find much to inspire you, with many ideas that you can easily adapt to your individual garden and needs.

Whatever your level of experience, this book is intended to help you achieve maximum pleasure from gardening.

WHAT IS LOW-MAINTENANCE GARDENING?

Low maintenance does not mean low impact. It means choosing surfaces and ground covers that do not require regular attention, and plants that remain within their allotted space and look good without regular pruning or hacking back. Plants are chosen that do not demand frequent feeding or require spraying almost as a matter of routine to control pests and diseases.

The amount of time and effort spent in the garden will reflect both the design and the choice of plants.

A low-maintenance garden of modest size may require only half an hour a week – probably less – to keep it looking really smart. If you go for a truly low-maintenance garden, which includes such drastic action as dispensing with the lawn, you should be able to go away on holiday for a few weeks and come back to something that looks as good on your return as it did on your departure.

There is little point in trying to achieve a formula that reduces work to a set amount of time, however, as you may enjoy doing some jobs – like planting and propagation – but resent others like weeding and watering. The amount of time your garden will take to maintain will depend not only on the time of year, but the size of your garden. Half an hour a week would be a long time for a very small garden, but a modest amount of time to spend keeping a large garden looking good.

A low-maintenance garden is one in which you never feel that keeping the garden shipshape is a chore. If you love pottering around with plants but hate mowing the grass, the simple expediency of

Above: *Some low-maintenance plants, such as heathers and dwarf conifers, are attractive the year round and need only occasional attention.*

Left: *Ground-cover plants, like this* Tiarella cordifolia, *look better than bare soil, and once established won't give weeds a chance to grow.*

replacing the grass with gravel or paving might be all that is necessary. If you quite enjoy the exercise involved in mowing the lawn but find the battle against pests and the need to prune or replant frequently tedious, then placing the emphasis on easy-care, no-fuss plants will probably be the best solution.

Take from this book those ideas that create the right combination of plants and hard landscaping with the amount of attention you want to give to your garden. If your garden then gives you pleasure without problems, this book will have achieved its aim.

Right: *Hard landscaping materials such as paving and gravel are a sensible alternative to grass if you want to cut down on the time and effort spent mowing and trimming edges. These needn't look uninspiring if you combine them with the appropriate plants.*

Labour-saving Tools

Appropriate tools can save you time and effort, and will make the difference between a job being a pleasure or a chore.

Good tools can be expensive and take up a lot of space, so decide which really will make life easier and spend as much as you can afford on a few good quality tools that will last, rather than purchase a lot of gimmicky tools that you'll seldom use. The suggestions here are arranged by task, and you probably won't need all of them. Decide which tasks create the most problems for you, then see whether one of these tools would help.

CHEMICAL CONTROL

If you decide to take the chemical route to low maintenance, a good compression sprayer will be well used. It will be invaluable in pest and disease control if you insist on growing old favourites that are prone to pests, such as roses and dahlias, but can also be used to apply foliar feeds and spray growth inhibitors that will reduce the frequency with which you have to cut your hedge.

A large-capacity compression sprayer with a long lance is much better for general garden use than a small hand-trigger sprayer. Choose a sprayer for which replacement parts are readily available.

It is not a good idea to use a compression sprayer for both weedkilling and other jobs. Not only could residues be left that will harm the plants, but damaging spray drift is more likely. Keep a watering-can just for applying weedkillers, and fit it with a dribble bar like the one on the watering-cans illustrated. It will apply the weedkiller evenly with the minimum of drift.

Above: *Dribble bars reduce the risk of spray drift, but it is still worth using a shield like this.*

Left: *Keep a watering-can fitted with a dribble bar for weedkilling.*

Far left: *Choose a pump-action compression sprayer with a long lance.*

CUTTING HEDGES

If your garden has a lot of hedge, a powered hedge trimmer will save a lot of time on what is a dusty and unpleasant job.

A mains electric trimmer is the best choice for most small gardens where the hedge is within easy reach of a power supply, but for a large garden a petrol model may be more practical. Battery-powered trimmers are useful for small hedges.

GRASS CUTTING

If you want to retain the lawn, the wider the cutting width of the mower, the faster you can cut the grass. Rotary hover mowers are light and easy to use, but if you worry about the clippings spreading all over the garden and house make sure you buy one with a clippings collector. The same applies to wheeled rotaries, which many people prefer. For a striped effect a cylinder mower with a rear roller is the best choice, although some other types now have rollers fitted to create a similar effect.

NYLON LINE TRIMMERS

A nylon line trimmer – the modern equivalent of a scythe – will make short work of long grass around trees, against fences and along edges, and many are able to produce a trim edge for the lawn much more quickly than traditional shears.

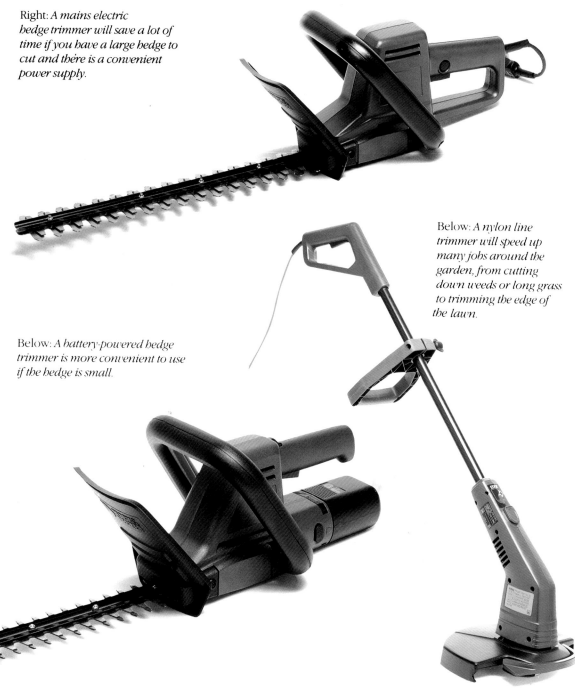

Right: *A mains electric hedge trimmer will save a lot of time if you have a large hedge to cut and there is a convenient power supply.*

Below: *A nylon line trimmer will speed up many jobs around the garden, from cutting down weeds or long grass to trimming the edge of the lawn.*

Below: *A battery-powered hedge trimmer is more convenient to use if the hedge is small.*

Automatic Watering

An automatic watering system will save you much time and is better for the plants, which are less likely to suffer from water stress. Some hoses, sprinklers and timing devices are described on the following pages, but these are just some of the systems that you can buy. Look at garden centres and in magazine advertisements to see which appear to be the most appropriate for your needs.

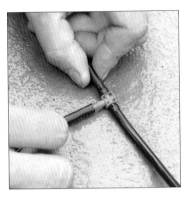

PLANNING THE SYSTEM

Work out the layout of your self-watering system first, and decide the number and kind of delivery devices (such as drip heads) you need. Kits are a useful start, but are unlikely to contain the exact number of components that you need. Check that the master unit or flow-reducer will support the number of drips required.

Above: *Most automatic watering systems are fitted with a suitable control system to reduce the pressure, and act as a filter. Designs vary, and either screw onto the outside tap or are inserted into the hose system. If the tap does not have a non-return valve fitted to prevent back-siphonage, make sure the master unit has one.*

Above: *Drip-feed systems are versatile enough to be used for plants in beds, borders or in containers. Use a T-joint to run branches or tubes for individual drip heads.*

Above: *Some automatic systems are controlled by the moisture level in the soil, but most operate on a continuous drip basis. Even if you can control the drip rate, too much water may be delivered if operated continuously. A timing device will turn your watering system on and off automatically, yet can easily be deactivated if the weather is bad. This one, operated by a battery, can be set to water your garden up to six times a day.*

Above: *Unless your garden is extremely small, it's best to install a pipeline buried just beneath the ground surface, then you can "plug in" various watering devices as necessary. With this particular system a sprinkler can simply be pushed onto the fitting set flush with the lawn or soil surface.*

Above: *Push the head onto the hose, and if necessary hold the delivery tube in position with a pipe peg. If the rate of delivery can be adjusted, the instructions that come with the kit will explain how this is done.*

Right: *An automatic watering device will keep your garden lush throughout the summer.*

Watering Aids

You may find the choice of watering aids bewildering, but decide what you want to water, then choose the kind of fitting that will do the job. You can avoid watering altogether if you choose drought-resistant plants, abandon containers, and don't mind a brown lawn in a dry summer. However, if you want lush, green grass and lots of colourful containers without the sometimes twice-daily chore of watering, some kind of automatic watering system is essential in the low-maintenance garden.

Above: *This type of drip feed is left connected continuously, through a flow-reducer provided, and the water-filled ceramic cone detects whether the soil is moist enough. Dry soil creates a partial vacuum, which then allows water to flow through the thin tubing, and the rate of flow can be adjusted. This system can be used in beds and borders but is ideal for troughs, tubs, and window-boxes. Like many drip systems, this one can also be fed from a reservoir or tank instead of being connected to the mains water supply.*

Above: *A drip-feed system is ideal for hanging baskets and window-boxes. Watering will probably have to be programmed to operate a couple of times a day – even in wet weather containers often need additional water because of the "rain shadow" created by the walls.*

Left: *Leaky-pipe and perforated hose systems are suitable for beds and borders or the kitchen garden. The special hoses are either porous or have many very fine holes, and water gradually seeps through them. You can bury them beneath the surface or lay them on top of the soil (useful where you might want to move the hose around).*

Right: *A pop-up sprinkler is ideal for a lawn. You don't have to keep setting it out, moving it around, and putting the sprinkler away afterwards. The pop-up sprinkler is set into the lawn, and the head is pushed up out of the ground by the water pressure when the tap is turned on. This can be done manually, or by a water timer.*

THE GARDEN FLOOR

The chances are that beds and borders form only a small part of your garden. The major part is probably devoted to flat surfaces such as lawns, paths, and paved areas. Lawns are labour-intensive and expensive to maintain, and plain paving can look boring, but there are many imaginative options that are neither hard work nor dull to look at.

Although paving is the surfacing material that usually comes to mind first, there are living alternatives to grass as well as choices such as gravel.

Low maintenance does not have to mean low interest, as these photographs show. These are just some of the ideas in this chapter that could be adapted for your own garden.

You can reduce the work involved in beds and borders simply by choosing suitable plants and keeping them weed-free with chemical controls or by mulching, perhaps with a decorative product such as chipped bark. But the garden floor – lawns and paving – may need a radical rethink.

Many people weary of cutting the grass think of paving as the obvious option. However, for many garden lovers the idea of a large expanse of boring paving sits uneasily with the soft lines and lush growth that is the traditional image of a beautiful garden. When paving fails, however, it is usually because it is used unimaginatively, or in a monotonous way.

If you use paving of different sizes and avoid rigid outlines, perhaps mixing it with other hard landscaping materials such as gravel, the effect can be dramatic and very pleasing. Gravel is a particularly useful material as it will conform to irregular outlines, but it can also be effective even in a

Top: *Gravel makes an attractive background for plants, and needs minimal maintenance.*

Above: *Curves present no problem for gravel.*

Right: *Paving is not dull if offset by attractive plants.*

Above: *Moss is a possibility for a shady problem area, but not suitable for a hot, dry site.*

Right: *If the design is strong and the garden well planted, a lawn will not be missed.*

small area that most people would pave. The town garden illustrated is packed with interest yet only needs the occasional five minutes work to keep it looking really smart.

There are living alternatives to grass, of course, and some of those, such as thyme and chamomile, are described later in this chapter. The shady Japanese garden illustrated above, however, shows that if you can't keep the moss out of your lawn there's something to be said for a moss "lawn" instead!

Lawns

A lawn is time- and energy-consuming but if you don't want to get rid of what is often the centrepiece of the garden, there are legitimate – and attractive – ways to reduce the frequency with which you have to mow.

Simply mowing different areas of the lawn to different heights, to create a textured effect can achieve a significant time saving but needs a fairly large lawn for the best effect. Naturalizing spring-flowering bulbs in a lawn of any size gives you the justification for leaving the grass uncut until late spring or early summer, when the leaves have died down.

A wild-flower lawn will bring many insect, animal and bird visitors to your garden, and regular mowing will be unnecessary. This kind of lawn can look untidy at times, so it's more suitable for the back garden than the front.

NATURALIZING BULBS IN GRASS

Choose bulbs that will multiply and flower freely, such as crocuses, daffodils, snowdrops, small fritillaries, and winter aconites. There are many different kinds of crocuses and daffodils, so you'll have plenty of choice even if you limit yourself to these particularly reliable bulbs and corms.

Above right: Hyacinth bulbs will make bold drifts if left undisturbed for several years, and there is the bonus of the flowers' fragrance.

1 For large bulbs, such as daffodils, scatter the bulbs randomly then make individual holes with a bulb planter (or use a trowel). Most bulbs planters are designed so that the core of soil is easily released.

2 Place the bulb into the hole, making sure there isn't a large air pocket beneath it, then return the core of grass. It may be necessary to remove a little soil from the bottom of the core for a snug fit. Firm the grass gently back into place.

3 For small bulbs or corms such as crocuses, you can lift an area of grass instead. Make an H-shaped cut with a spade blade or edging tool, and fold back the turf. Then fork in a little slow-acting fertilizer such as bonemeal.

4 Scatter the bulbs or corms randomly and leave very small ones where they fall. Larger ones may need planting with a trowel. Level and firm the soil, then return the grass. Firm it in carefully to ensure the ground remains level.

A WILDLIFE HAVEN

You can encourage birds, butterflies and other creatures by having a wild-flower lawn instead of a conventional lawn. You may still want to retain a grass lawn for practical purposes, but some of the area can be allowed to "go wild", especially if the area is not on public view.

1 The most satisfactory way to make a wild-flower lawn is to sow a special wild-flower mixture instead of lawn seed. Be sure to remove problem perennial weeds first.

2 To bury the seeds, simply rake first in one direction and then in the other. It does not matter if some seeds remain on the surface. Keep the area well watered until the seeds germinate.

3 For a very small area, you may prefer to buy wild-flower plants, which are now sold by some garden centres. You can also raise your own plants, starting them off in seed trays or pots.

4 You can plant into bare ground or put them in an area of lawn left to grow long. Don't forget to keep them well watered until established.

Above: *An area like this, full of wild flowers, can look drab at certain times of the year, but is enchanting when the plants are in bloom.*

THE ANNUAL HAIRCUT

A wild-flower lawn cannot simply be left uncut, or it will become an untidy wilderness. Cut the area down to within a few centimetres (inches) of the ground in the autumn or when most of the flowers have finished blooming and have shed their seeds. This will make it look tidier for the winter, and new growth next spring will not become entangled with old growth.

Cut the Mowing Time Down to Size

There's a lot you can do to keep mowing time to a minimum. It may be necessary to buy a new and better mower, but just cutting out fussy beds, and curved edges might simplify and speed things up by allowing you to mow up and down in straight lines. Or you can take a sideways look at the problem and cut different parts of the lawn at different intervals, leaving some areas longer.

KEEP A STRAIGHT LINE

Beds cut into the lawn will probably increase mowing time. Although they reduce the area of lawn, the inability to mow up and down in straight lines will probably slow you down. Creating a striped finish is particularly difficult and beds also create more edges to trim. Consider filling them in with grass or at least making them into rectangles.

KEEP A STRAIGHT EDGE

Untrimmed edges can make a garden look untidy, but trimming with long-handled shears – or especially with ordinary shears – is tedious and time-consuming.

If you have a lot of lawn edges to trim, buy a powered lawn edger, or choose a nylon line trimmer with a swivel head that can be used for this job as well as scything down weeds.

Above: *A curved bed will add considerably to mowing time, as you will not be able to mow in a straight line.*

Above: *A nylon line trimmer will enable you to trim edges with considerable speed.*

MULTI-LEVEL MOWING

Another way to cut down on the mowing for a large lawn is to create a "sculptured" effect. Keep the broad "pathways" cut regularly, cut other areas with the blade set higher, and mow only every second or third time. Leave some uncut except for a couple of times a season. However, do remember that very long grass can't easily be cut with a mower; you need to get out your nylon line trimmer.

Above: *If the lawn is large, try leaving the grass in part of it to grow long. Wild flowers will start to thrive, and you will only need to cut it once a year.*

MAKE A MOWING EDGE

If you have a mowing edge like this, edge-trimming will be required much less often. If the edging is set level with the grass, the mower, which is run onto the edging, will trim off the long grass at the edge. You may still have to trim any spreading grass stems that grow over the paving, but this will only be necessary occasionally.

1 Lay the paving slabs on the grass for positioning, and use a half-moon edger (edging iron) to cut a new edge.

2 Slice off the grass with a spade, and remove enough soil for a couple of centimetres (inches) of sand and gravel mix, mortar, and the slabs. Consolidate the sub-base.

3 Use five blobs of mortar on which to bed the slab, and tap the paving level, using a mallet or the handle of a club hammer.

4 Make sure the slabs are flush with the lawn, and use a spirit level to check that the slabs are laid evenly. Mortar the joints for a neat finish, otherwise weeds will grow in them.

Above: *Bricks can be used instead of paving slabs, and in a formal setting these can give an attractive crisp finish to the bed.*

CUT WIDE, SAVE TIME

Next time you buy a mower, think about the cutting width. Wider mowers cost a little more but will save time. But think carefully first – if your lawn is very small the saving may not be significant and the extra manoeuvrability of a smaller mower can be important if there are few long straight runs.

Alternatives to Grass

If you like a green lawn, but don't enjoy the regular grass cutting, why not try a grass substitute? None of those suggested here will stand up to the hard wear of a children's play area like grass, but just for occasional foot traffic and as a feature that is for admiration only, there are some practical alternatives that don't need regular mowing.

THYME

Thyme is aromatic when crushed, and makes a good grass substitute, but don't use the culinary thyme (*Thymus vulgaris*), which is too tall. Choose a carpeter like *T. pseudolanuginosus* or *T. serpyllum*.

CHAMOMILE

Chamomile (*Chamaemelum nobile*, syn. *Anthemis nobilis*) is also aromatic and looks good too. Look for the variety 'Treneague', which is compact and does not normally flower.

CLOVER

If clover is a problem in your lawn, it may make a good grass substitute. Once established it will keep green for most of the year, and will tolerate dry soils. You'll only have to mow a couple of times a year, after the flowers appear, to keep it looking smart. You will need to order clover seed from a seed company that sells wild or agricultural seeds.

PLANTING A THYME LAWN

You must prepare the ground thoroughly and eliminate as many weeds as possible otherwise weeding will become a tiresome chore. Time spent now will be time saved later.

1 Prepare the ground thoroughly by digging over the area and levelling it at least a month before planting. This will allow the soil to settle and weed seedlings to germinate.

2 Dig out any deep-rooted perennial weeds that appear. Hoe out seedlings. Rake level again.

3 Water all the plants in their pots first, then set them out about 20 cm (8 in) apart, in staggered rows as shown (a little closer for quicker cover, a little further apart for economy but slower cover).

4 Knock the plant from its pot and carefully tease out a few of the roots if they are running tightly around the edge of the pot.

5 Plant at their original depth, and firm the soil around the roots before planting the next one.

CHEAP PLANTS

Pot-grown plants from a garden centre can be expensive if you need a great number. You can cut the cost by buying some plants and using these for cuttings. Grow them on for a year before planting. Some thymes are easily raised from seed, but start them off in seed trays then grow on in pots for a season.

BEWARE THE PITFALLS

Grass substitutes have drawbacks as well as advantages. You won't be able to use selective lawn weedkillers on them, so it's back to old-fashioned hand weeding. Once the new lawn is well established and the plants have knitted together this will not be a major problem, but weeding will be a chore for the first season or two.

Beware of common stonecrop (*Sedum acre*), an attractive yellow-flowered carpeter sometimes sold as a grass-substitute. It looks great, but it will probably become a serious weed in your garden. You will almost certainly regret its introduction.

6 Water the ground thoroughly and keep well watered for the first season.

Right: *Thymes make an attractive alternative to grass if the area is small and is unlikely to take much wear.*

Gravel Gardens

Gravel is great if you want an easy-to-lay, trouble-free surface that looks good and harmonizes well with plants. It's worth getting to know your gravels, especially if you're looking for practical alternatives to a lawn.

Right: *Many garden centres and stone merchants sell, or can obtain, a wide range of gravels in different sizes and colours. You will find the appearance changes according to the light and whether the stones are wet or dry.*

MAKING A GRAVEL GARDEN

Gravel is an easy and inexpensive material to work with, and a small gravel garden can be created in a weekend.

Below: *Gravel gardens can be a formal or informal shape, but an edging of some kind is required otherwise the gravel will become scattered into surrounding beds.*

1 Excavate the area to a depth of about 10 cm (4 in), with a slight slope to avoid waterlogging after heavy rain. If the gravel garden is low-lying or in a hollow, provide a sump for excess water to drain into.

2 Make sure the surface is reasonably smooth, then lay thick plastic sheeting over the area (to suppress weed growth). Overlap the joints.

3 Tip the gravel over the plastic sheet, and rake it level. It is difficult to judge how deeply or evenly the gravel is being spread once the plastic sheet has been covered, so if necessary scrape back the gravel occasionally to check progress.

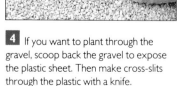

4 If you want to plant through the gravel, scoop back the gravel to expose the plastic sheet. Then make cross-slits through the plastic with a knife.

5 Make the planting hole with a trowel, enrich the soil with garden compost and fertilizer and plant normally. Fold back the sheet, and replace the gravel without covering the crown if it's a small plant.

Paving

Paving won't look boring if you choose attractive slabs. You could use clay pavers that match the house or surrounding raised beds, and soften them with suitable plants.

A paved area needs practically no maintenance – just an occasional brush and perhaps a clean with a high-pressure sprayer every three or four years to bring back the fresh look. Paving should always be balanced with low-maintenance plants to avoid it looking bleak and harsh. It is also important to choose materials that blend in with the rest of the garden, so that they add to the sense of design.

LAYING PAVING

This method of laying paving is also suitable for bricks.

1 Always lay paving on a firm base. Excavate the area to a depth that allows for hardcore, mortar, and paving. Firm the ground, then add 5–10 cm (2–4 in) of hardcore for foot traffic, about 15 cm (6 in) if vehicles will use it. Compact the ground thoroughly.

2 Bed the slabs on five blobs of mortar, using five parts of sharp sand to one part cement.

3 Alternatively, you can lay the slabs with a solid bed of mortar, although this will make it more difficult to adjust them.

4 Start at a known straight edge, then position each slab in turn. The best way is to lower the slab down from one side, then slide it if adjustments are necessary.

Left: Builder's merchants will stock a variety of paving materials, so choose those that will complement existing elements in the garden.

CLAY PAVERS

Clay pavers cannot be bedded on mortar like paving slabs and bricks. They are usually designed to interlock without mortar joints and are intended for bedding on sand.

5 Tap the slab level with a mallet or the handle of a club hammer, using a long spirit level that spans adjoining slabs. If a large area of paving is being laid, it may be necessary to lay it on a slight slope to drain rainwater, in which case you must allow for this.

6 Unless the slabs are designed to be butt-joined, use spacers to ensure a gap of consistent width. You can make these from scraps of wood. A few days after the slabs have been laid, point with mortar.

Right: *This paved area is softened by the addition of container-grown plants.*

Plants and Paving

Make your paved areas more interesting by mixing materials, and leaving plenty of space for plants. That way it will always remain high on impact and still low on maintenance.

PLANTING IN PAVING

A large expanse of paving needs some plants to soften the effect. Keep containers to a minimum unless you have an automatic watering system. Instead, try lifting a few paving slabs and plant straight into these prepared areas. The effect will be similar but with much less commitment than containers demand.

MIX AND MATCH MATERIALS

Paving often looks a more integrated part of the garden if you combine it with raised beds or low walls made from the same or matching materials – but always check that bricks used for walls are suitable for paths as well.

Using the same or matching paving for paths and patios is another way of giving your garden a more integrated look.

If the area is large, try mixing materials. Using two or three different materials usually works well, but more than three is likely to look confused. Try bricks or clay pavers with timber, or railway sleepers, or natural or man-made paving slabs. You could perhaps leave out some areas of paving and fill them with gravel or pebbles.

Above right: This paved area is combined with a raised bed made from contrasting materials.

1 Lift one or two paving slabs, using a cold chisel or bolster with a club hammer to break the mortar and lift the slabs.

2 Remove the mortar and any hard-core, then fork in several buckets of garden compost or a proprietary planting mix, together with a handful of slow-release fertilizer.

3 Plant the shrub normally, firming the soil around the roots and watering thoroughly. Keep well watered in dry weather for the first season.

4 Beach pebbles or gravel may be used to cover the soil and make it look more attractive. This also reduces the chance of soil splashing onto the paving.

ADDING PEBBLE TEXTURE

1 Beach pebbles (you can buy these from some builder's merchants, garden centres and stone merchants) are a good way to create an area of different texture. Leave out as many slabs as appropriate and fill the area with a dryish mortar mix. Then lay the stones close together.

2 If the area is likely to be walked over, make sure the stones are flush with the surrounding paving. Use a stout piece of wood laid across adjoining slabs to ensure they are flush and reasonably level. Press them further into the mortar if necessary. Spray lightly with water if the mix is too dry, and clean any mortar off the stones.

Right: *Mixing materials breaks up a large area of the garden and prevents it from looking dull.*

BEDS AND BORDERS

Hard surfaces like paving and gravel are low maintenance, but do not make a garden. Beds and borders are what clothe a garden and make it pleasant, but they are also potentially time-consuming. It is the plants that you grow in your beds and borders that will largely determine how much time you have to spend keeping your garden looking good.

Try to avoid using plants that grow rampantly, those that need constant cutting back or frequent pruning, and any with lots of seeds that germinate readily.

Shrubs are among the best plants for borders, though you still have to choose with care. Most shrubs will grow for years without any attention once they have become established, but those that grow too vigorously (such as the butterfly bush and many roses, both of which require annual pruning to look good), or tall and difficult to manage (like lilacs), are probably best avoided. If you want to avoid annual pruning, even popular favourites such as forsythia and japonica are best omitted, especially if you like your plants to look neat and tidy and remain reasonably compact.

There are so many well-behaved, beautiful shrubs to choose from that a low-maintenance shrub border is easy to achieve.

A garden of shrubs alone inevitably looks rather too predictable. Although flowers come and go, and perhaps there's a final moment of glory as leaves colour before they fall, the overall shape and texture of a shrub border remains fairly constant. For that reason it's a good idea to use some herbaceous plants, either in their own border or mixed with the shrubs.

Herbaceous border plants have a reputation for being high

maintenance, with staking, cutting down, and dividing being an almost annual ritual with some of them. Simply avoid these and choose those that you can plant and forget (at least for a few years). Plants like astilbes, dicentras, and bergenias (the latter is a

Above: *Mixed borders generally require less maintenance than herbaceous borders, especially if annuals are kept to a minimum and the emphasis is on low-maintenance shrubs. Easy perennials like these* Penstemons *help to add a touch of colour.*

Below: *Well-filled borders can help to soften the harsh outline of rectangular paving.*

Right: *A tree at the back of the border adds both height and colour, yet involves no routine work.*

non-woody evergreen) need no staking, spread relatively slowly and are easy to pull up or restrain when the time comes.

A bed of grasses can be very striking, but always be cautious about mixing grasses among other plants, as some species are difficult to control.

Most trees are also very low maintenance, and can be integrated with shrubs, but they should always be chosen with care. Plant only trees that are likely to remain in proportion to the size of your garden.

Both shrubs and herbaceous plants can be used for weed-suppressing ground cover in beds and borders, and these can be great allies, for bare soil is bad news for a low-maintenance gardener.

Gravel Beds

Gravel makes a splendid back-drop for plants, and it's easy to keep weed-free. Dwarf alpines and large 'architectural' plants like yuccas or red-hot pokers look equally good. The plants that look best in a gravel bed, however, are those that naturally grow in dry or stony conditions.

You were shown how to lay an area of gravel as an alternative to grass or paving on pages 24–5. You can plant in any area of gravel, but if you want to make a feature where plants predominate, you may prefer to set the feature in an area of grass, as shown here.

GRAVEL BEDS IN GRASS

You should be able to find space for a gravel bed like this even in a small garden.

1 Mark out the bed with rope, a hose, or by sprinkling sand where you think the outline should be. If the lawn is large, a long and winding ribbon of gravel can look very effective. This is sometimes referred to as a dry-riverbed style. If the garden is smaller, a more compact shape, perhaps oval or kidney-shaped might be more appropriate.

Above: *A gravel bed will make an excellent setting for a variety of plants, such as this sedum.*

2 Cut the outline of the bed using a half-moon edger. A spade will do, but this does not produce such a crisp edge.

4 Spread a generous quantity of garden compost or rotted manure over the surface, and a slow-release or controlled-release fertilizer. Then fork this in to loosen and enrich the soil. If the ground is poorly drained and you want to grow "dry soil" plants, work in plenty of coarse grit too. This is an important stage as it is difficult to improve the soil once the gravel is in place.

3 Lift the grass within the bed with a spade, removing about 10 cm (4 in) from the surface. The finished bed must be a couple of inches below the grass, otherwise the gravel will spill onto the lawn and damage the mower.

5 Spread about 5 cm (2 in) of gravel over the soil, making sure it is kept off the lawn and does not threaten to spill over onto it.

PLANTS TO USE

Although many plants will grow well in a gravel bed, for a low-maintenance garden you should choose drought-resistant plants that you won't need to water, even in dry spells.

PLANTING

To plant, just draw back the gravel in that area and plant normally, but avoid planting deeply as the gravel will be drawn back around the plant afterwards. For most plants this will do no harm, but if necessary just keep the gravel away from the immediate area around the stem.

6 Try adding a few boulders or beach pebbles. These create interest and make the bed look more natural.

Right: *A gravelled area. Gravel beds can be heavily planted with a combination of drought-resistant plants and the weed-suppressing gravel will mean they mainly look after themselves.*

Herbaceous Borders

Herbaceous plants need to be chosen with care. Some well-behaved, no-fuss but showy plants are suggested here but there are many more. If in doubt, always find out whether the plant needs staking, how fast it spreads and whether it is prone to pests and diseases. Border phlox and perennial asters are prone to mildew, for example.

PLANTING A BORDER

After the initial planting, your border will need little care to keep it looking good.

1 Always make sure the pots have been watered before planting, otherwise the root-ball may remain dry as water runs off it when watering after planting.

2 Space the plants out in their pots before you start to plant, as changes are easy at this stage. Try to visualize the plants at their final height and spread, and don't be tempted to plant them too close.

3 Knock the plant out of its pot only when you are ready to plant, so that the roots are not exposed unnecessarily to the drying air. Carefully tease out some of the roots.

4 Plant small plants with a trowel, large ones with a spade, and always work methodically from the back, or from one end of the border.

5 Return the soil and make sure the plant is at its original depth or just a little deeper. Firm it with your hands or a heel to expel large pockets of air in the soil.

6 Water thoroughly unless the weather is wet. Be prepared to water regularly in dry weather for at least the first few weeks after planting.

RELIABLE AND EASY PLANTS

It's worth including some of the following plants on your shopping list, but add others to suit the size of your border and to reflect your own taste.

Agapanthus (not for cold areas)
Alchemilla mollis (may self-sow so be prepared for seedlings)
Anemone hybrida
Anthemis tinctoria
Astilbe
Bergenia (a non-woody evergreen)
Catananche caerulea
Dianthus (a non-woody evergreen)
Dicentra spectabilis
Echinops ritro
Erigeron
Hemerocallis
Kniphofia
Liatris spicata
Lilium (not if lily beetles are a problem in your area)
Liriope muscari
Polemonium caeruleum
Schizostylis coccinea
Veronica spicata

GARDENER'S TIP

You can buy pot-grown herbaceous plants at any time of the year, but spring or autumn are the best times to plant.

Right: *Herbaceous borders will need less care if you plant large clumps of fewer kinds rather than lots of different ones that will need more frequent attention.*

Mixed Borders

Don't be too rigid about the plants that you use or mix in beds and borders. Herbaceous and non-woody evergreens can be useful ground cover around shrubs, while some shrubs, such as rue, can often be mistaken for herbaceous plants when used among them. Sometimes a mixed border containing both shrubs and herbaceous plants can bring out the best in both. If there are any gaps left because the plants are still small, don't hesitate to sow some bright annuals instead of leaving bare soil for weeds to colonize.

Above: *This very narrow bed shows how charmingly shrubs and herbaceous plants may be combined. However, if slugs are a problem in your garden, you may find the hostas an unwise choice.*

Above: *Hostas have been planted at the front of this mixed border. The height differential means that you have the benefit of two borders in one, as the hostas in front do not mask the tall plants behind.*

Right: *Plants such as* Astilbe *and* Potentilla *add colour to mixed borders and can largely be left to their own devices.*

Astilbe chinenis pumila

Potentilla *'Tangerine'*

Right: *This narrow border is only about 1.2 m (4 ft) wide, but herbaceous perennials have been allowed to tumble over at the front to provide useful colour contrasts with the yellow shrub behind. This is the evergreen* Choisya ternata *'Sundance' with* Aster novi-belgii *'Audrey' (left) and 'Jenny' (right) and a pink chrysanthemum in the centre. In front is a pink-flowered rock rose that would have bloomed in late spring and early summer. This kind of combination of shrubs and herbaceous plants ensures season-long colour.*

Using Grasses

A grass lawn can be high maintenance, but a grass bed can make a striking feature that will not take up much of your time. Grasses can also be used in mixed beds and borders, but be careful as some of them will make a take-over bid for territory and can be difficult to eradicate if entwined with other border plants. Choose well-behaved clump-forming species or plant in a container as shown below.

PLANTING GRASSES

Groups of grasses are refreshingly different, but beware of the rampant species.

3 Firm the soil around the roots, using your hand or heel, then water in thoroughly. Keep watered in dry spells until the plants are well established.

4 If planting a spreading grass in a border, or even if using a rampant species in a grasses-only bed, plant it in a large pot or container to restrain its spread. This method is not suitable for very large grasses, but you are unlikely to be using these in a small border. Excavate a hole large enough to take the container, which must have drainage holes in it.

1 Grasses often work best as a low-maintenance feature in a bed of their own. There are many kinds to grow, from compact dwarfs for the edge to huge plants 2.4 m (8 ft) or even taller. Study a specialist catalogue, and when you have bought the plants space them out to see how they will look.

2 Make sure the plants have been well watered beforehand, then knock out of the pot and plant in well-prepared, weed-free soil. If there are a lot of roots tightly wound around the edge of the pot, gently tease out some of them.

5 Partly fill the container with soil then plant normally, with the rootball at the correct level. Firm the plant well, and add more compost if necessary.

6 Make sure the rim is flush with the surrounding soil (but not below it, otherwise the most rampant grasses will escape), and for a more natural appearance make sure that the soil is flush with the rim. Water thoroughly.

Right: *Grasses can be attractive plants to use in a border. Some can be used as an edging but most are used mid- or back-border.*

Fern Gardens

Most people dismiss garden ferns as boring and uninteresting, but anyone who has grown ferns as houseplants will know how fascinating and beautiful they can be. What they lack in colour they make up for in elegance.

Don't be deterred from trying garden ferns if you have had trouble keeping indoor ferns happy and healthy. Provided they have suitable conditions (shade for most of them), they will thrive without any help on your part.

Use ferns in a shady position where the more colourful flowers fail to thrive. If you are worried about bare ground in winter, choose mainly evergreen species, but a mixture of shapes and sizes will make your fern garden more interesting.

PLANTING A FERN GARDEN

Ferns are easy to grow but most prefer a moist, shady or partially shaded position, and it pays dividends to prepare the ground thoroughly. Spring is a good time to plant.

Dryopteris pseudomas 'Cristata' *(king fern)*

Asplenium Scolopendrium *(Hart's-tongue fern)*

1 Most ferns need a moist, humus-rich soil, so fork in as much garden compost or rotted manure as possible. This is especially important if the area is shaded by trees or a wall that also casts a "rain shadow", where the soil is usually dry.

2 If the soil is impoverished, add a balanced fertilizer and rake it into the surface. If planting in late summer, autumn or winter, do not use a quick-acting fertilizer. Wait until spring to apply, or use a controlled-release fertilizer that will only release the nutrients when the weather is warm enough for growth.

3 It is very important that ferns do not dry out, especially when newly planted. Water the pots thoroughly about half an hour before planting, to make sure the rootball is wet to start with.

Left: *Experiment with different combinations of types of foliage when choosing ferns.*

4 Make a hole large enough to take the rootball, but if the roots are very tightly wound around the pot, carefully tease out some of them first. This will encourage them to grow out into the surrounding soil. If the plant is in a large pot, you may have to use a spade instead of a trowel.

5 Firm in carefully to eliminate any large air pockets that could allow the roots to dry out. Then water thoroughly so that the surrounding soil is moist down to the depth of the rootball.

Right: *Because ferns are subtle rather than bright, they can be used very effectively to soften a focal point like this ornament. This simple combination can transform an otherwise potentially dull corner of the garden.*

6 To help conserve moisture and maintain a high level of organic material in the soil, mulch thickly with peat, a peat substitute or a garden compost. Top up the mulch each spring.

Easy Bedding

If you like the cheerful brightness of seasonal bedding rather than the permanent but predictable show from shrubs and border plants, you can compromise by using a mixture of seasonal and permanent plants. This will reduce the amount of regular replanting and save on cost as well as time.

If you do want to use traditional summer bedding plants, choose those that flower prolifically over a long period without deadheading. Some of the most trouble-free and spectacular bedding plants to use are suggested opposite.

PLANTING A PERMANENT EDGING

Perennials will form the basis of the edging, with bedding plants added for variety.

1 Always dig over the ground and clear it of weeds before planting.

2 Rake in a general fertilizer before planting. (Wait until spring to apply the fertilizer if planting in autumn or winter.) This will encourage vigorous early growth and help the plants to knit together more quickly.

BE ECONOMICAL WITH THE ANNUALS

These pictures show how imaginatively you can use summer bedding plants in combination with perennials. The plants you choose should reflect your own preferences, but the concept is easy to adapt to your own needs.

3 Space out the plants in their pots first, in case you have to adjust them to go evenly around the bed.

4 Plant with a trowel, adjusting the spacing to suit the plant. About 15 cm (6 in) apart is suitable for most plants if you want quick cover, further apart if you don't mind waiting a little longer for a carpeting effect.

5 Firm in to remove large pockets of air, then water thoroughly. Keep well watered for the first few weeks. The bed may be planted immediately with spring or summer bedding plants or bulbs as appropriate. When they have finished, lift them but leave the perennial edging.

Begonia
'White Devil'

Impatiens
(busy lizzie)

Left: Impatiens *(busy lizzie) and begonias are popular choices for colourful beds.*

NO-FUSS SUMMER BEDDING PLANTS

The following will continue to flower for many months without deadheading, regular attention or watering.

Begonia semperflorens
Impatiens (busy lizzie)
Lavatera trimestris
Osteospermums
Pelargoniums (bedding geraniums)
Petunias
Tagetes patula (French marigolds)

Right: *This edging is the perennial* Sedum spurium *'Album Superbum', but many other carpeting plants can be used (beware of very invasive sedums, however). This provides a neat year-round edging that you don't have to replace and at most needs an annual trim to keep it neat. Fill the centre of the bed with spring and summer bedding plants.*

Heathers

Heathers make excellent low-maintenance beds, with a guarantee of evergreen cover and – depending on the varieties used – colourful flowers practically the year round. Many have attractive golden foliage that looks good for twelve months of the year.

Use them with dwarf conifers if you want to add height, or alone for a carpet of living colour. You could use them as a ground cover around the base of a birch tree with silver bark – winter-flowering varieties will look stunning.

Calluna vulgaris 'Blazeaway'

PLANTING A HEATHER BED
Prepare the soil thoroughly as some heathers have special needs. Although heathers will suppress weeds after they have been established for a couple of years or so, you will have to control weeds for the first few seasons.

1 Dig the soil thoroughly, and pull up as many deep-rooted or difficult perennial weeds as possible. Add plenty of organic material such as garden compost or rotted manure, especially if the soil is dry or impoverished.

2 If planting in spring or summer, rake in a balanced general fertilizer. If planting in autumn or winter wait until spring to apply fertilizer.

Erica carnea

Above: *A combination of heathers, such as* Erica carnea *and* Calluna vulgaris, *will provide interesting colour variations, even when not in flower.*

3 Some heathers, such as the winter-flowering *Erica carnea* varieties will grow on a neutral or even slightly alkaline soil. Many others, such as *Calluna vulgaris*, need an acid soil. Adding peat to the planting area will benefit all types.

4 Start planting at one end or at the back of the bed. Space the plants about 30–45 cm (12–18 in) apart, but the planting distance will vary with species and even variety, so check first.

5 Use a mulch to help suppress weeds, conserve moisture, and improve the appearance of the bare soil while the plants are still young. Peat is useful for this, but you may prefer to use a renewable alternative such as chipped bark.

Above: *Heathers make happy companions for conifers, and if you choose winter-flowering varieties like these* Erica carnea, *the garden will always be bright.*

PLANTING THROUGH PLASTIC

This method will cut down weeding to the absolute minimum.

1 Cover the whole area with black plastic or a plastic mulching sheet. Make cross-shaped slits in the plastic.

2 Plant through the slits in the sheet.

3 If you don't like the visual appearance of the plastic, cover it with a mulch of chipped bark.

Dwarf Conifers

Dwarf conifers need practically no attention after their first year, but to look effective they are best grown as a group with contrasting shapes, sizes and colours, or with colourful carpeters such as heathers.

PLANTING A CONIFER BED

A good garden centre will have a bewildering array of dwarf and slow-growing conifers, but it is best to consult a good specialist catalogue or book before you buy. Some described as dwarf may reach 2.4 m (8 ft) or so in time, and those described as slow-growing may be even larger eventually. Make sure your dwarf conifers really are dwarf if space is at a premium.

Chamaecyparis obtusa *'Aurea'*

Chamaecyparis lawsonia *'Silver Threads'*

Above: *These varieties are among many that need little care, but provide year-round colour.*

1 Dwarf conifers look good in a small bed or border. If you find it difficult to plan beds and borders on paper, stand the pots where you think the plants will look good, and be prepared to shuffle them around until they look right. Bear in mind the eventual height and spread.

2 Dig a hole larger and deeper than the rootball. Stand the pot in the hole to make sure it is large enough.

3 Fork in as much rotted manure, garden compost, or planting mixture as you can spare. This is especially important on very dry soils, or near a fence or wall.

4 Add a controlled-release or slow-release fertilizer to the planting hole, using the manufacturer's recommended rate, and work in with a fork or trowel.

5 Make sure the soil in the pot is moist, then knock the plant out and check the roots. If they are very tightly wound around the inside of the pot, carefully tease some of them out so that they will grow into the surrounding soil.

6 Check the planting depth by standing the rootball in the hole, and using a cane or piece of wood to make sure it will be at its original depth when the soil is returned. Add or remove soil as necessary.

Right: *This bed shows how bright and colourful a conifer and heather bed can be, and it really is a low-maintenance combination.*

7 Firm in to eliminate large air pockets that might cause the roots to dry out, then water thoroughly.

8 Mulch with a decorative material such as chipped bark. Make sure the mulch is at least 5 cm (2 in) thick so that it will suppress weeds effectively.

Combining Heathers and Conifers

Heathers and dwarf conifers are low-maintenance plants that you can use alone. But they also go well together, with conifers providing useful height and variation in shape, and heathers supplying seasonal colour.

DESIGNING THE BED

Although you can make a one-sided border, an island bed is much more pleasing. The heathers are also likely to thrive better in a more open position with plenty of sun all day.

You could design a bed for year-round interest. There are hundreds of suitable heathers and dwarf conifers that you could use, so modify the bed to suit the size of your garden and the plants available at your garden centre.

Planting a bed like this might seem expensive initially, but bear in mind that it will probably last for decades without the need for replanting. It's a small price to pay for a really interesting, long-term, minimal-maintenance feature.

Above right: *Newly planted heathers can look small and insignificant, but within a year or two will merge into each other and into the conifers. Avoid overcrowding.*

Opposite: *Heathers and conifers make a happy marriage, one enhancing the other.*

PLANTING A MIXED BED

A mixed bed like this will provide interest but will entail no extra upkeep.

1 Arrange the conifers first, making sure they look pleasing from all angles. Move them around if you are not satisfied at first. Prepare the ground well, as described on page 44. Plant the conifers first, firming them in before watering.

MASS PLANTING

Heathers look best planted in bold drifts. A group of perhaps ten or twenty plants of one variety will have far more impact than the same number of different varieties planted in the same area. Unless the bed is large, choose perhaps half a dozen good varieties but plant plenty of them. This applies to both foliage and flowering varieties.

2 Space the heathers out around the conifers. Plant in groups or drifts of one variety at a time. Avoid planting too close to the conifers as both the conifers and heathers will spread.

3 The bed will look more attractive initially, while there is still a lot of bare soil, if you mulch with chipped bark, or gravel.

Self-sufficient Shrubs

Some of the most popular shrubs – like roses and buddleias – need a lot of attention if they are to remain looking good. Pruning is a regular requirement for many of them, and those prone to pests and diseases are bad news unless you are prepared to spend time spraying or dusting too. But for every shrub that is a potential problem for the low-maintenance gardener, there are many more that are just as attractive and almost totally trouble-free.

There are hundreds of well-behaved compact shrubs that will not demand frequent pruning or hacking back. If in doubt, check with your garden centre to make sure the shrubs you choose don't need regular pruning, won't become bare and leggy at the base with all the flowers at the top, and aren't susceptible to diseases.

PLANTING SHRUBS

Shrubs will be in position for many years, so take your time over planting and prepare the ground thoroughly.

1 Water the pots thoroughly and let them drain, then position them where you think they should be in the border. Check the likely size on the label or in a book, then revise your spacing if necessary. If the spacing seems excessive initially, you can always plant a few extra inexpensive shrubs between them to discard when they become overcrowded.

2 Fork over the area, and remove any weeds. Then fork in as much rotted manure or garden compost as you can spare, or use a proprietary planting mix.

3 Excavate a hole large enough to take the rootball. Stand the pot in the hole and use a cane or stick to check that the plant will be at its original depth in the soil when planted. Add or remove soil as necessary.

4 Carefully tease out some of the roots if they are tightly wound around the inside of the pot. This will encourage them to grow out into the surrounding soil more quickly.

5 Return the soil and firm it well around the roots to steady the shrub in wind and to prevent large pockets of air that might allow the roots to dry out. Pressing the earth in with your heel is the most effective way of firming the soil around a shrub.

6 Apply a balanced fertilizer according to the manufacturer's instructions, if planting in spring or summer. Hoe or rake it into the surface, then water thoroughly.

Right: *A border like this is planted with* Choisya ternata *'Sundance' a low-maintenance shrub, and Michaelmas daisies, yet it remains bright and beautiful for many months of the year.*

SELF-SUFFICIENT FLOWERING SHRUBS
Cistus
Escallonia
Hibiscus syriacus
Hypericum
Mahonia
Olearia × haastii
Yucca

SELF-SUFFICIENT FOLIAGE SHRUBS
Aucuba japonica
Berberis thunbergii
Choisya ternata
Elaegnus pungens 'Maculata'
Euonymus fortunei
Ruscus aculeatus
Viburnum davidii

Make the Most of Trees

Trees largely look after themselves, and make attractive features as specimens set in a lawn, or planted towards the back of a shrub border.

Trees in a border are generally less trouble because falling leaves drop almost unnoticed onto the soil and are quickly recycled. Leaves on a lawn usually have to be raked up, and mowing beneath a low-hanging tree or up to a trunk can also cause difficulties. Don't be deterred from trying a tree in a lawn, but choose one with small or evergreen leaves, and try some of the tips suggested below to make mowing and cultivating around the base easier.

TREES IN LAWNS
Mowing will be frustratingly difficult if you take the grass right up to the trunk of the tree, especially as it becomes larger. Lawn trees are generally better planted in a bed cut into the grass, which you can plant with some of the ground cover plants suggested for borders, or cover with a decorative mulch to suppress weeds.

TREES IN BORDERS
The best way to cover the ground beneath trees in a border is with ground cover plants that will tolerate shade and dry soil. If the tree is very large, or has large leaves, you may have to rake them off the plants when they fall, but most of them usually work their way between the plants and soon rot down. If you use a ground cover that dies down in winter, falling leaves will not matter.

HOW TO PLANT A LAWN TREE
Trees often look best planted in isolation in a lawn.

1 With sand, mark a circle on the grass about 90–120 cm (3–4 ft) across. Lift the grass with a spade, and remove about 15 cm (6 in) of soil with it. Fork in as much garden compost or manure as possible.

2 Insert a short stake before you plant, placing it on the side of the prevailing wind. Place it off-centre, to allow space for the rootball. A short stake is preferable to a long one.

3 If planting a bare-root tree, spread out the roots. Place the tree in the hole and use a cane to check that the soil mark on the tree's stem will be at final soil level, about 5 cm (2 in) below the grass.

4 Return the soil, and firm in well. Water thoroughly and secure with a tree-tie. Use a thick ornamental organic mulch to suppress weeds and make the bed look more attractive.

Right: *Once established* Hedera colchica 'Dentata Variegata' *will form an attractive evergreen carpet that will suppress weeds and needs practically no attention.*

Left: *Use beach pebbles instead of an organic mulch to make an attractive feature. They will prevent weed growth and can look very ornamental.*

A RAISED EDGE

Raising the edge makes more of a feature of the bed, but you won't easily be able to mow up to the edge unless you also make a mowing strip. A sunken border about 10–15 cm (4–6 in) wide all round will enable you to mow over the edge without striking the raised edge.

Flowers that Sow Themselves

Plants that germinate readily from self-sown seeds can be a problem in the wrong place, but you can use them freely in areas that have a natural boundary, such as a bed in a lawn, or around a tree or shrub. You will have to sow them initially.

Right: *These* Aquilegia alpinum *have sown themselves, and all the gardener had to do was a little thinning and weeding in the spring.*

HOW TO START THEM OFF

Decide on a position where the plants can multiply freely without becoming a nuisance. Suitable places are among shrubs and herbaceous plants, especially in a mixed bed, or in beds restrained by clear boundaries. Don't sow them where you will have to keep weeding out the seedlings where they're not wanted.

SELF-SOWING ANNUALS

Calendula (pot marigold)
Eschscholtzia (Californian poppies)
Limnanthes (poached egg plant)
Linaria (toad flax)

SELF-SOWING PERENNIALS

Aquilegia (columbine)
Lupinus (lupin)
Foeniculum vulgare (fennel)
Digitalis (foxglove) (a biennial)

1 Start with weed-free ground. Hoe off or pull out any weeds in the area you want to sow. Fork out any deep-rooted perennial weeds.

2 Annuals used for this purpose are best scattered randomly rather than sown in rows. Avoid sowing too thickly otherwise you'll have more thinning to do.

3 Perennials, like lupins and columbines, should be sown in small pinches about 45 cm (18 in) apart, instead of being scattered randomly.

4 Simply rake the annual seeds in, first in one direction and then the other if possible. Pull some soil over the perennials sown in spaced pinches. Keep watered until they germinate and are growing well.

5 After initial sowing, and each subsequent year, pull out any weed seedlings before they compete with the sown seedlings. You should be able to identify the desirable seedlings by the larger number with the same kind of leaf.

6 As the seedlings become larger, hoe between them to control weeds. Once the plants meet, you should be able to stop weeding.

Make the Most of Bulbs

Some bulbs will flower reliably year after year with the clumps improving all the time. Whether it's spring-flowering daffodils, summer alliums, or autumn colchicums, there are plenty of bulbs that you can plant and forget.

Most summer-flowering bulbs, such as alliums and lilies are best planted in groups in a border, but the easiest way to grow many spring-flowering and autumn-flowering bulbs is to naturalize them in the grass. Don't cut the grass until the leaves die down (colchicums flower in autumn but the leaves do not appear until spring).

NATURALIZING LARGE BULBS
Tulips and daffodils can be planted in this way.

1 To create a natural effect, scatter the bulbs on the grass and plant them where they fall. It is better to keep your naturalized bulbs to one small area of the lawn so that the rest can be cut normally and it won't look too untidy.

2 You can plant with a trowel, but a bulb planter is quicker and more convenient. Insertion will be easier if the ground is moist.

3 Crumble some soil from the bottom of the core. Drop some of this into the hole to fall around the bulb and make sure it is not suspended in a pocket of air. Then press the core back into position.

NATURALIZING SMALL BULBS
Plant snowdrops or crocuses in the lawn for spring flowering.

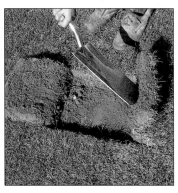

1 For small bulbs and corms it is sometimes easier to lift and then replace the grass. Use a half-moon edger, or a spade, where you want to lift the grass. Use a spade to slice beneath the grass, then roll it back for planting.

2 Loosen the soil with a fork, and work in a slow-acting fertilizer such as bonemeal.

3 Scatter the bulbs randomly. Very small ones can be left on the surface; larger ones are best buried slightly. Aim to cover the bulbs with twice their own depth of soil under the grass. Roll back the grass, firm it well, and water.

DIVIDING ESTABLISHED CLUMPS

Naturalized bulbs and those left in a border for many years will eventually need dividing to prevent overcrowding, which will lead to deteriorating results.

1 Lift very large clumps when the leaves have just died back, or any time when the bulbs are dormant.

2 Separate the clump into smaller pieces and replant. You do not have to separate into individual bulbs.

Right: *Naturalizing bulbs in grass eliminates the need for annual re-planting and means you don't have to cut that part of the lawn until the leaves have died down naturally!*

Living Carpets

Ground cover is one of the labour-saving gardener's best weapons. It suppresses weeds, covers bare soil, and makes a really worthwhile visual contribution. Some of the flowering kinds of ground-cover plants are both colourful and beautiful.

Right: Convallaria majalis *(lily-of-the-valley) takes a few years to become established, but then makes an effective as well as a fragrant ground cover.*

NON-WOODY GROUND COVERS

Ajuga reptans (E)
Alchemilla mollis
Anthemis nobilis (E)
Bergenia species (E)
Cerastium tomentosum (E)
Geranium endressii
Lamium maculatum
Pulmonaria species
Tiarella cordifolia (E)
Waldsteinia ternata (E)

(E) = evergreen

PLANTING GROUND COVER

Ground cover will eventually suppress weeds, but initially needs protection from them.

1 Clear the ground of weeds first. Annual weeds can be hoed off or killed with a herbicide. Some perennial weeds will have to be dug out by hand or killed by several applications of a translocated weedkiller, as regrowth occurs.

2 Fork in as much rotted manure or garden compost as you can spare, then apply a slow-release or controlled-release balanced fertilizer at the rate recommended by the manufacturer, and rake it in.

3 Unless planting a ground cover that spreads by underground stems or rooting prostrate stems on the surface, it is best to plant through a mulching sheet to control weeds while the plants are becoming established.

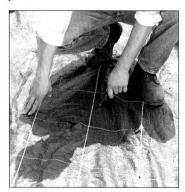

4 Spread out the mulching sheet. Using scissors or a sharp knife, cut a cross where the plant is to be positioned. Plant in staggered rows, at spacings appropriate for the plants.

5 Provided you use small plants, it should be easy to plant through the slits with a trowel. If using large ground-cover plants it may be better to omit the mulching sheet and plant with a spade.

6 Be sure to water thoroughly after planting, and in dry weather throughout the first year.

7 It will probably take several seasons before the plants knit together to form a living carpet so, although not essential, you may prefer to use a decorative mulch such as chipped bark to improve the overall appearance.

Shrubby Ground Cover

Many shrubs and sub-shrubs are compact enough to be used as ground cover. Some will make impenetrable thickets that will take on the toughest weeds; others – including ground-cover roses – are less effective at weed control but deserve to be planted for their beauty.

BE IMAGINATIVE

Conifers can make a very pleasing ground cover, but you may have to be patient because although a single plant may have a spread of 3 m (10 ft), it may take some years to get there!

Heathers are among the most popular flowering ground covers, and once established only require a trim with shears after flowering. Unfortunately they can become woody in time and may require replacing after some years.

Some cotoneasters grow into large upright shrubs, but some, such as *C. dammeri* and *C. conspicuus* 'Decorus' are ground-hugging and make excellent ground cover in front of other shrubs.

Some shrubs, such as *Hypericum calycinum*, are really too rampant for normal ground cover in a small garden. But this hypericum is ideal for a sloping bank that would otherwise be difficult to cultivate, or where its spread is limited by an area surrounded by paving.

Many thymes make attractive ground covers, but choose a prostrate kind such as *T. serpyllum* rather than the more bushy *T. vulgaris* which is used as a culinary herb.

EVERYTHING'S ROSY

Roses sound an unlikely form of practical ground cover, and some of the earlier types used for the purpose could be disappointing. Nowadays, however, there are very compact, ground-hugging kinds that are well worth trying where you want something beautiful as well as weed-suppressing.

Below: Ground-cover shrub roses will not provide year-round cover, but are difficult to beat for impact while they are in bloom.

Right: Prostrate cotoneasters are useful ground cover shrubs.

Dealing with Difficult Positions

Don't write off unpromising positions as unsuitable – there are even ground-cover plants for heavy shade and dry soil. These are usually foliage plants but they will look much better than bare soil or weeds. Provided you are prepared to water them until they are well established, you can then leave these plants to their own devices.

MULTIPLY AND SAVE MONEY

If the cost of buying the quantity of plants required for ground cover deters you, try multiplying your stocks and making the most of your investment.

If you need a lot of plants it may be possible to raise them from seed. *Cerastium tomentosum*, *Alchemilla mollis*, aubrietas, and thymes are among the ground-cover plants easily and quickly raised from seed. Many others can be divided or cuttings taken. Often you can buy, say, a third of the plants required, and divide them up (or take cuttings) to provide the number of plants needed. You will start with small plants, of course, and cover will be slower, but you will cut down on cost.

PLANTS TO GROW BENEATH TREES
Convallaria majalis
Galeobdolon argenteum
Hedera helix (and other ivies)
Liriope muscari
Pachysandra terminalis
Vinca minor

PLANTS FOR SHADE
Epimedium grandiflorum
Galeobdolon argenteum
Hedera helix (and other ivies)
Hosta
Pachysandra terminalis
Vinca minor

PLANTS FOR DRY SOIL
Acaena novae-zelandiae
Armeria maritima
Cotula squalida
Hebe pinguifolia 'Pagei'
Helianthemum nummularium
Thymus serpyllum

Right: Hedera canariensis *'Variegata' creates an attractive ground cover beneath trees.*

MULTIPLYING PLANTS

You will have to wait for complete ground cover, but multiplying plants in this way will result in substantial savings.

Right: *Many spring-flowering bulbs can be depended on to produce a reliable display in shade, but they may deteriorate over the years if the light is too poor.*

1 Some shrubby ground cover plants that spread by underground runners or suckers – such as *Pachysandra terminalis* – can easily be divided into smaller pieces. A plant like this can easily be divided into three or four plants. Water first to make sure the potting soil is moist.

2 Knock the plant out of its pot. If it doesn't pull out easily, try tapping the edge of the pot on a hard surface.

3 Carefully pull the rootball apart, trying to keep as much potting soil on the roots as possible.

4 If you find the crown too tough to pull apart, try cutting through it with a knife. It is better to do this than damage the plant even more if it does not separate easily.

5 It has been possible to divide this plant into eight smaller ones, but the number you will be able to achieve depends on the size of the original plant and the species.

6 Replant immediately if you don't mind small plants, otherwise pot up and grow on for a year before planting.

7 Pot up the plants if you want to grow them on, using a good potting mixture. Keep them in a sheltered but light position, and make sure they never go short of water.

8 If you don't have automatic watering, plunge the pots up to their rims in soil. They will dry out less quickly and watering will not be such a chore.

EASY-CARE CONTAINERS

Plants in containers imply a high commitment of time and effort as watering can be a twice-daily chore in very warm weather. So the only sensible way to use seasonal bedding plants in containers in a low-maintenance garden is to install an automatic watering system. Even that leaves you with the cost and effort involved in replanting perhaps twice a year.

The other approach is to grow tough plants such as shrubs and some dwarf conifers, which are much more tolerant of neglect.

You do not have to forego containers, however, as there are plenty of plants that are not so prone to premature death if watering is neglected for a day or two, and that are less demanding about tasks such as deadheading. These are perennial plants that can remain in their containers for several years – sometimes for perhaps 10 years or more in the case of trees and shrubs – before repotting becomes imperative.

You won't have such a colourful and prolonged show as summer bedding plants will produce, but as focal points they can be just as successful.

Above: *A standard holly like this will give many years of trouble-free beauty for minimal effort.*

Right: *This collection of shrubs, conifers, and bergenia have plenty of impact, yet they will give years of beauty and won't die if you forget to water them for a day or two.*

Far left: *Spring-flowering plants such as primroses, crocuses and dwarf irises will brighten up a dull spot, but keep to just a few containers as they will require regular attention.*

Left: *Instead of planting all the containers with seasonal bedding, it helps to use some planted with shrubs that do not demand regular replanting, and that are reasonably tolerant of dry compost.*

Shrubs for Containers

Shrubs have plenty of potential as container plants for the low-maintenance garden. Not only will you save time on regular replanting, but many are also much less demanding regarding watering. It's still highly desirable to water daily in summer, but if you can't fit an automatic watering system they probably won't come to much harm if you neglect them for just a day or two.

Remember, if you want a shrub on a patio, it's better to lift a paving slab to create a planting area so that watering is even less critical, but use a container for places where there's no alternative.

MIXED COLLECTIONS

If a single-subject tub sounds unappealing, try a mixed planting of, say, three small shrubs. One combination might be a spiky pinkish-red phormium, a grey-leaved bushy plant such as *Santolina chamaecyparissus* or *Helichrysum italicum*, and perhaps a hebe with green leaves and blue or purple flowers. Mix and contrast shapes and colours.

The phormium is unsuitable where the winters are cold, but you could use a dwarf upright purple berberis, such as *B. thunbergii* 'Helmond Pillar', instead.

FINISHING TOUCHES

Evergreens such as camellias and rhododendrons are spectacular in flower, but a trifle boring for the rest of the time. A decorative pot will make sure these plants always remain a feature. Adding fine gravel or stone chippings to the surface also helps to make them more decorative.

PLANTING SHRUBS IN CONTAINERS

Shrubs can seem expensive container plants but bear in mind that they will give you years of pleasure if you plant properly.

Fatsia japonica

Aucuba japonica

1 Shrubs need a large container, with a diameter of at least 30 cm (12 in). Always make sure that an ornamental ceramic pot is frost-proof. Place pieces of broken pot in the bottom, or if that's not possible use coarsely chipped bark.

2 Half-fill with a loam-based potting soil as shrubs need the weight and stability, and the better nutrient-holding capacity of this kind of mixture.

3 Remove the tree from its container and try it for size (it may be necessary to remove some of the potting soil to lower it). Carefully tease out some of the thick roots running around the edge, then trickle soil around the rootball.

4 Always firm the potting soil well, as a leafy shrub will offer a lot of wind resistance. Then water thoroughly.

Left: Aucuba japonica *and* Fatsia japonica *also make attractive shrubs for containers.*

Right: *Rhododendrons make good container plants if you choose a compact variety. Later they can be planted in the garden if they become too large.*

Potted Perennials

Border perennials are seldom used in containers, but if you have a town garden with no space for a proper herbaceous border, you might like to try some of your favourite plants in tubs and troughs. Provided you choose plants that are not too tall, and which don't normally need staking, it's worth trying them. The flowering period is often short, so it's best to choose plants that also have attractive foliage.

Although it sounds a contradiction in terms, some herbaceous border plants are evergreen – though they are more accurately described as non-woody evergreen perennials. You won't have to keep replanting the containers, but you will need to divide and replant every second or third year. And of course they still need watering regularly, so if possible install an automatic watering system.

BE IMAGINATIVE
Choose a plant that is long-lasting in flower, like *Polygonum affine* and *Lychnis coronaria*. If it also has interesting foliage, like the lychnis, so much the better.

Foliage plants like *Houttuynia cordata* 'Chameleon' will remain colourful and attractive for longer than most flowering plants. Other good foliage border plants to try are *Hakonechloa macra* 'Alboaurea', and *Carex morrowii* 'Evergold', as well as the many variegated hostas.

Some border plants, like dicentra, have the added advantage of both pretty flowers and attractive foliage.

PLANTING A PERENNIAL TROUGH
Although the following steps show you how to plant a trough, the same principles apply to window-boxes and even tubs.

Hosta fortunei

Houttuynia cordata 'Chameleon'

1 Troughs should be deep and hold as much potting soil as possible, to support perennial plants. Always insert a layer of broken pots or coarsely chipped bark for drainage.

2 Partly fill the trough with a nutritious potting soil. Those that are loam-based will be less prone to drying out than those based on peat, and have better reserves of nutrients for long-term plants like perennials.

3 If planting a mixed collection, position the plants in their pots first, and be prepared to move them around until they look right. Place ground-huggers at the front so that they can trail over the edge.

4 Make sure the soil in the pots is moist then start planting from the back or one end. Firm them in well, making sure the tops of the rootballs are covered with soil so that they are less likely to dry out.

Left: *Hostas and a foliage plant such as* Houttuynia cordata *are a good choice for containers.*

Right: *For best results, choose plants with contrasting or bold, coloured foliage. It is worth adding one or two short-term flowers, like this lily, to add variety.*

Seasonal Highlights

Permanently planted containers may lack the excitement of variety. You can overcome this by leaving space for a couple of small pots when you do the initial planting, then placing a few colourful flowers into these spaces, changing them as each one passes its best.

WINTER AND SUMMER INTEREST

This tub has been planted mainly with evergreens that will remain clothed the year round. The red skimmia berries remain attractive from autumn through to spring, and the ajuga looks particularly good when growing vigorously and cascading over the edge in summer. To make a planting like this work throughout the year, space has been left to insert a pot for additional seasonal colour. Here an impatiens has been used for summer colour. In the autumn this will be replaced by a pot of winter-flowering pansies, followed by snowdrops for late winter, then early irises such as *I. danfordiae*, and then primroses. Pansies can be used to fill the gap until it is safe to insert an impatiens again.

Vary the plants to suit your own preferences, but use the principle of a permanent planting and replacing just one or two pots of short-term plants as necessary.

PLANTING FOR REPLENISHMENT

You can prevent your perennial containers from becoming boring by planning for a little seasonal variety.

1 When planting, insert an empty pot and plant around it. A 7.5 cm (3 in) or 10 cm (4 in) pot is adequate, as suitable flowers are often sold in these sizes.

2 Firm the potting soil around the empty pot, so that it leaves a pot-shaped mould when you remove it.

3 Use this mould to house a pot of seasonal flowers. You can insert the pot directly if the size is right, but watering will be more demanding. It is usually better to knock the plant out of its pot first.

4 Insert the rootball and firm the soil around it. If necessary, trickle some fresh potting soil around the edge to pack any gaps. Once flowering has finished and the plant looks unattractive, remove it and replace with something different. It will usually just lift out, otherwise use a trowel to loosen it.

WINTER BASKET

Winter baskets are usually a failure. Even tough plants suffer or die as the exposed soil becomes frozen solid from all sides. But you can make a colourful winter basket that doesn't even need regular watering!

Line the basket with a moss or foam basket liner, then cut florist's foam to fit the basket. Make sure it is moist then push evergreen foliage into the florist's foam until you can't see the basket itself.

For colour, be sure to include some berries and, if possible, a few long-lasting winter flowers such as heathers. This basket contains *Euonymus fortunei* 'Emerald 'n' Gold' and 'Emerald Gaiety', *Elaeagnus pungens* 'Maculata', *Erica hyemalis* in flower, and holly and pernettya berries.

Water periodically to keep the florist's foam moist.

Above: *This winter basket was made from flowers and foliage cut from the garden, and inserted into moist florist's foam. This kind of winter arrangement will last for many weeks.*

Left: *Only one plant in this container is seasonal, but the bright red impatiens makes itself the centre of attraction.*

SMART IDEAS

There are many ways to reduce the amount of time spent maintaining the garden, and it's worth asking yourself what features you want and whether there are ways to enjoy them without a heavy commitment.

Hedges can cause much anguish, but for many of us a living hedge is preferable to a fence or wall. With a little imagination, you may be able to overcome the problem by cutting the hedge in a different way, or even uprooting the old one and replacing it with an alternative that is easier to maintain, without sacrificing the appearance of the garden, or having to resort to a brick wall.

Climbers are popular for softening walls and fences, but these too can become time-consuming to keep looking smart if you constantly have to tie and train. The answer is to choose climbers and wall shrubs that can be planted and left largely to their own devices.

Water can be low-maintenance too, and a large pond may be less trouble than a flowerbed. If you like ponds, using water may be one way to create an interesting low-maintenance garden.

Growing vegetables can be very satisfying, but you will have to question yourself seriously about which ones to grow, and how. If you want a low-maintenance garden to include vegetables, try some of the tips suggested on pages 80–81.

Right: A pond like this will become a strong focal point, yet the amount of maintenance required is modest. It may be necessary to rake rampant submerged plants, and to divide old plants, occasionally.

Above: *Hedges can be beautiful as well as practical, like this* Berberis × stenophylla.

Right: *Use plants imaginatively, like this* Clematis macropetala *softening an area of wall and paving.*

Using Water

Overcrowded plants benefit from division and replanting in spring, and in autumn it's best to cut down dead foliage that might pollute the water, and to rake out most of the leaves that fall in. Apart from that, however, ponds are very low on maintenance. They don't require cleaning out annually, although it is worth giving them a spring clean every second year.

MAKING A LINED POOL

You can make this in a weekend. The only hard part is excavating the hole.

1 Make your pool as large as possible – it will make a better feature, the fish and wildlife will be happier, and the water will probably stay clearer. Start by marking out the shape with a hosepipe or rope.

PLANTS FOR PONDS

Iris laevigata (Japanese iris)
Pontederia cordata (Pickerel weed)
Aponegeton distachysos
(Cape pondweed)
Acorus graminens 'Variagatus'
(grassy-leaved sweet flag)
Juncus effusus 'Spiralis'
(Corkscrew rush)
Myriphyllum aquaticum
(parrot's feather)

2 Excavate the soil to the required depth, but leave a shallow ledge about 23 cm (9 in) down around part of the pond. This is for plants that require shallow water. If you are having a paved edge, remove enough grass for this, remembering to allow for the mortar bed as well as the thickness of the paving. It is essential to check the levels all round. Use a spirit-level in all directions.

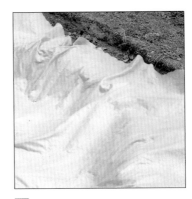

3 Remove any sharp stones or large roots, then line the pool with a 12 mm (½ in) layer of sand (it will stick to the sides if damp). If the soil is very stony, use a polyester mat (sold by water garden suppliers) instead of sand.

4 Drape the liner loosely over the excavation, with an overlap all round. Hold the edges in place with a few bricks, then fill with a hosepipe.

5 As the weight of the water takes the liner into the pool, lift the bricks periodically to allow the liner to mould easily into the excavation. Try to remove some of the worst creases as the water fills, but don't expect to be able to eliminate all of them.

6 Once the water has reached its final height, trim off the surplus liner, leaving a 15 cm (6 in) overlap all round. Lay the paving on a bed of mortar, trapping the edge of the liner. Make sure the paving overlaps the edge by an inch or two, so that any drop in water level is not so noticeable.

PLANTING A POND

The best time to plant aquatics is spring and early summer.

1 Use a planting basket designed for aquatic plants, and line it with a special basket liner made for the purpose (or use a piece of horticultural fleece cut to size). Plant in garden soil or an aquatic soil. Do not use a potting soil intended for ordinary pots as this will contain too much fertilizer.

2 Cover the surface with gravel. This will reduce the chance of the water becoming muddied when placing the basket in the pond, and should also deter fish from stirring up the soil.

3 Most waterlilies should be planted in deeper water, but miniature waterlilies and all the "marginal" plants should be placed on the planting shelf at the edge.

Above: *A raised patio pool like this makes an eye-catching feature for a small garden. You can also use a liner to waterproof this kind of pool.*

Beating the Hedge

Hedges can be a chore. They are dusty and tiring to cut, and too frequently they are a trifle boring and over-large into the bargain.

Lifting and replanting a hedge is a big job, but there's a lot you can do to make lighter work of it once it is established. Buying a suitable electric trimmer of appropriate size, reducing the surface area to be cut, and even using a growth retardant, will all make life easier.

If you're feeling energetic and planning for the future, you might want to consider replanting with an attractive flowering or foliage hedge that might provide less of a barrier but will look brighter and won't demand maintenance or clipping so often.

Right: *You can sometimes improve the shape of a straight-sided hedge by sloping the sides, which will also marginally reduce the amount of hedge to be cut. Sloping sides can better withstand a heavy snowfall and allow more light to reach to the base of the hedge on each side.*

Very wide hedges can sometimes be reduced in width, but if it's a boundary hedge you should talk to your neighbour first. The best way to reduce the width is to insert painted canes – to make them easier to see – 30 cm (1 ft) further in than you want the final edge to be, to allow for new growth.

Cut back to the markers. If the stems are thick and tough, you may need a saw or long-handled pruners instead of secateurs. This is best done in winter or early spring for deciduous hedges, and in late spring for evergreens. A year later, trim the new growth back to the desired width.

Left: *A low height and tapering sides will make cutting easier and quicker.*

CHEMICAL PRUNING

If you have a formal, clipped quick-growing hedge that you want to keep looking smart without having to trim too often, look for a growth regulator sold for the purpose. These are sprayed onto the hedge after trimming, to inhibit further growth of the leading shoots. A few long shoots may grow out from within the hedge, but are easily trimmed off. You can spray your side of the hedge without affecting growth on your neighbour's side.

Not all hedges are suitable for this treatment, and they must be over three years old. You must spray on a calm day to avoid spray drift. Read the manufacturer's instructions carefully, and bear in mind the cost and time involved in spraying.

Right: *You may be able to save time on hedge-trimming by reducing the area to be cut. If your hedge is 1.8 m (6 ft) tall and 60 cm (2 ft) across, reducing the height to 1.2 m (4 ft) will reduce the amount of hedge to be cut by around 30 per cent. This saving alone is significant, but the top of a 1.2 m (4 ft) hedge is also easier to cut than one 60 cm (2 ft) higher, for which you may need steps.*

Many established hedges will respond to quite severe height reduction. But remember that you should cut back to about 30 cm (1 ft) lower than you want the final height, to allow for new growth.

LONG BLADE, SHORT TRIM

A powered hedge trimmer is essential if you want to cut down on the time and effort involved in clipping hedges. If the hedge is very small, consider a trimmer that operates from a rechargeable battery rather than struggle on with hand shears.

For a large hedge, think about blade length. A 60 cm (2 ft) blade will knock a third off the cutting time in comparison with a 40 cm (16 in) blade. However, a longer blade means more weight and the trimmer will probably be more tiring to use, so you may prefer a blade length between the two as a compromise.

Self-supporting Climbers and Shrubs

Climbers that need regular pruning, training or tying are best avoided, no matter how beautiful they may be. There are plenty of others that will clothe a wall with the minimum of attention. If you like more demanding plants like clematis and roses, try growing them the natural way – through other shrubs.

PLANTING A CLIMBER

Climbers need special care when planted in the dry soil near a wall or fence.

1 The soil close to walls and fences, or other shrubs and trees, is usually dry because of the "rain shadow" created. Always make the planting hole at least 45 cm (1½ ft) away, and work plenty of moisture-holding material such as garden compost or manure into the soil.

2 Plant at an angle so that the stems grow towards the wall. Leave in any cane that was used as a support while in the pot, but if there are several stems untie them and spread them out a little.

3 Self-clinging plants will not require a trellis and will cling without help. But to start it off when newly planted, use small ties that you can fix to the wall by suction or a special adhesive.

4 Water thoroughly, not only after planting but whenever the ground is dry for the first season. The roots can usually find moisture once well established, but are vulnerable initially.

Right: *Some climbers like this* Clematis montana rubens, *can be trained over ropes, to produce a garland effect.*

Left: *Some climbers such as clematis and roses can be allowed to grow naturally through another shrub or into a tree. You can even let these two plants grow through each other.*

Time-saving Kitchen Garden

The kitchen garden is usually labour-intensive, with many hours spent digging, levelling, watering, feeding and weeding. If you want to grow fruit and vegetables in a low-maintenance garden, choose those less demanding of attention and try some of the labour-saving tips suggested here.

WATERING

Vegetables need plenty of water, so install a sprinkler. Add on a time switch if you want to make it even more automatic.

Seep hoses are ideal for rows of vegetables as the water is directed to where it's needed.

BLACK OUT THE WEEDS

You can almost eliminate weeding by using a mulching sheet that will keep out light yet let through water. Although this method is unsuitable for plants sown *in situ*, most vegetables put out as plants can be grown this way.

Always make sure the soil is enriched with manure or garden compost and fertilizers before you lay the sheet. Later feeding is best done by applying a liquid fertilizer.

1 Make a slit trench around the edge of the area, and tuck the edge of the sheet into this. Pull the soil back over the edge.

2 Make planting slits with a knife, at the spacings normally used for the particular vegetable you are planting.

3 Plant through the slits, using a trowel. Don't forget to water in thoroughly.

EASY POTATOES

Potatoes grown conventionally require a lot of attention, including earthing up several times. Lifting them also involves heavy digging. Reduce the work involved in growing potatoes by planting beneath a black polythene sheet.

1 Prepare the ground, then cover with polythene. Make a slit in the soil around the edge and tuck the sheet into this. Pull the soil back over the edges.

2 Make planting slits with a knife, and plant through these using a trowel. Follow the spacing normally recommended for the variety of potato.

3 When the plants are ready for harvesting (which is when the tops start to die down), simply lift the sheet and pick them from the surface.

SOWING AIDS

If you find spacing by hand difficult, one of the proprietary seed-sowers might help. Seed-sowers are available for both seed trays and drills, but you will have to bend to use them. A long-handled sower is more convenient for the vegetable garden.

FRUITS TO GROW AND AVOID

Give strawberries a miss – they look and taste good but are very demanding. Concentrate on soft fruit such as blackcurrants and raspberries. Gooseberries are less trouble than strawberries, but they are prone to pests and diseases so avoid them if you aren't prepared to keep an eye on them.

Rhubarb is as trouble-free as anyone could want. You can leave it for years, to flourish without any attention at all.

It's best to avoid tree fruits such as apples and pears, which are prone to problems and demand careful pruning if trained to one of the systems popular in small gardens. If you want an apple tree, try one of the flagpole types that grow upright and form the fruit on natural short spurs along the upright stem. Apart from cutting out the odd wayward shoot, you can forget about pruning.

Right: *A productive kitchen garden need not be labour-intensive.*

WEEDING AND FEEDING

There can be few gardeners for whom weeding is not a chore, and most of the low-maintenance gardener's efforts are aimed at relegating weeding to a very occasional task. Whether you tackle the problem with hard landscaping such as paving, or use dense planting, you really can have a beautiful garden where weeds are seldom a problem. If you don't give weeds space, they are unlikely to gain a major hold.

With modern fertilizers, feeding is also less of a chore than it used to be.

It is an irony that in feeding your plants you are also feeding the weeds. But if you get the weeds under control from the start, all the nutrients that you apply will be available to the desirable plants, and the weeds will not be competing for nutrients or light.

The art of mulching is something to be learnt by anyone interested in low-maintenance gardening. It suppresses weeds and helps to keep the ground moist. If you choose an organic mulch, it will also rot down gradually, thus increasing soil structure and fertility.

Right: *Gravel makes an attractive surface, and contrary to popular belief is easy to keep weed-free with minimal effort.*

Above: *Mulching will reduce the need to water so often, and it will suppress weeds.*

Right: *To keep a herbaceous border healthy like this, you must be prepared to feed, but an annual spring application of a balanced fertilizer should be sufficient.*

Sheet Mulches

Mulches fall into two main groups: the mainly inorganic ones made from various forms of plastic or rubber sheets, and loose ones such as garden compost and chipped bark that will eventually rot down and add to the humus content of the soil.

"Loose" mulches are described on pages 86–87. Both have their uses, and you may want to add one of the more decorative loose mulches to make a sheet mulch visually more acceptable. This can be more cost-effective than using a loose mulch alone, which has to be applied at least 5 cm (2 in) thick to be an effective weed control.

MULCHING WITH A SHEET
Use this method for low-maintenance shrub beds and newly planted trees.

1 Sheet mulches are most useful in shrub beds that can be left undisturbed for some years, and are best used when the bed or border is newly planted. Always prepare the ground as thoroughly as you would if not using a mulching sheet.

Make a slit around the edge of the bed with a spade, and push the sheet into this. For a vegetable plot you can use special plastic pegs, but these are too conspicuous for an ornamental position.

2 Make cross-shaped planting slits in the sheet with a knife or scissors. If planting a shrub you will probably have to make slits large enough to take a spade for planting. This won't matter as the sheet can be folded back into place.

3 Small plants can be planted with a trowel, but for shrubs you will need to use a spade. Provided the ground has been well prepared before the sheet was laid, it should be easy to dig out the planting hole.

4 Sheet mulches are very useful around newly planted trees and shrubs. The best way to apply the sheet is to cut a square or circle to size, then make a single slit from the centre. Place it around the tree or shrub – and the stake if there is one – and simply fold it back into place. It won't matter if the join is not perfect as you can hide it with a decorative mulch.

5 Although most of the sheet mulch will be hidden as the plants grow, it will be very conspicuous initially. A layer of a decorative mulch such as chipped bark or gravel will make it much more acceptable.

Black polythene is inexpensive and widely available. It does not allow water to penetrate, so it's best used in narrow strips, alongside a hedge.

Although more expensive than polythene sheets, woven plastic mulches allow water to seep through while keeping out light.

Butyl rubber is a very long-lasting waterproof mulch. It is expensive, but you only require a thin gauge. It is more suitable for the area immediately around trees than as cover for a large area.

Some sheet mulches are made from degradable materials such as wool waste. This is a good option if you want a sheet mulch that will eventually disappear as it rots.

Below: *Established plants are more difficult to mulch with a sheet, but trees and hedges can be mulched this way very satisfactorily. If you want to control weeds along a young hedge, lay black polythene in two strips, one either side of the hedge.*

PRACTICAL POINTS

- Always prepare the soil thoroughly before laying the sheet.

- Enrich the soil with plenty of organic material such as rotted manure or garden compost – you won't have an opportunity later.

- Add fertilizer and water it in thoroughly – only liquid feeds are practical once the sheet is in position.

- Soak the ground before applying the sheet.

Above: *Sheet mulches can look unattractive in the ornamental garden. They are better covered with a shallow layer of a decorative mulch too.*

Loose Mulches

Most loose mulches are visually more acceptable, and the organic ones gradually rot or become integrated into the soil by insect life and worm activity, thus helping to improve soil structure and fertility.

Loose mulches have to be thick to suppress weeds well. Aim for a thickness of about 5 cm (2 in).

APPLYING A LOOSE MULCH

1 Prepare the ground thoroughly, digging it over and working in plenty of organic material such as rotted manure or garden compost if the soil is impoverished.

2 Loose mulches will control annual weeds and prevent new perennial ones getting a foothold. You must dig up deep-rooted perennial weeds, otherwise they could grow through the mulch.

chipped bark

3 Water the ground thoroughly before applying the mulch. Do not apply a mulch to dry ground.

4 Spread the mulch thickly. This is bark mulch, but there are other decorative mulches that you could choose from.

gravel

peat

Material

Chipped bark

Cocoa shells

Garden compost

Gravel

Peat

Rotted manure

Sawdust

Spent hops

Spent mushroom compost

Advantages

Very ornamental, and lasts for a long time before it needs replacing

Light to handle. Attractive colour and pleasant smell when handling. Lasts for a long time

Excellent soil conditioner. High level of nutrients. Free if you make your own

Visually pleasing. Long-lasting

Visually pleasing and pleasant to handle. Very useful for plants that require acid conditions

Excellent soil conditioner. Useful nutrient levels. Can be inexpensive if you have a local source

Usually cheap if you have access to a plentiful supply. Usually slow to decay

Usually quite inexpensive if you live in an area where they are readily available. Easy and pleasant to handle

Usually relatively inexpensive. Should contain animal manure and straw, which will improve the soil

Disadvantages

Can be relatively expensive. May take some nitrogen from the soil as it rots down

Can be relatively expensive. Sometimes can encourage growth of superficial moulds

Soon breaks down, which enriches the soil but means you need to keep topping up. Not visually attractive

Contains no nutrients. Individual pieces may be a problem if they get onto the lawn

Relatively expensive. Low in nutrients. Many people prefer to avoid its use because its extraction depletes peat reserves and peat bog habitats

Soon breaks down, which enriches the soil but means you need to keep topping up. Not visually attractive, and can smell if not thoroughly rotted

Can temporarily deplete the soil of nitrogen when rotting down. Can be visually pleasing when newly applied but soon looks unattractive

Can be difficult to obtain, especially in small quantities

Normally contains lime, so should be avoided on alkaline soils or where acid-loving plants are grown

Controlling Weeds

The only place where weeds are acceptable is in a wildlife corner, although some people find daisies in the lawn a very attractive feature. Generally, however, weeds have to be controlled, and pulling them up by hand is a tedious and time-consuming job that few of us enjoy. It's even more frustrating if they grow again within days.

There are two main weapons if you want to cut down on weeding: mulching, which uses no chemicals, and herbicides – or weedkillers if you prefer to use a more descriptive term!

KILLING WEEDS IN BEDS AND BORDERS

Although there are weedkillers that will kill some problem grasses growing among broad-leaved plants, generally you can't use selective weedkillers in beds and borders. Most weedkillers will kill or damage whatever they come into contact with, but there are ways in which you can use herbicides around ornamental plants to minimize the amount of hand weeding necessary.

2 You may be able to treat areas in a shrub border with a watered-on weedkiller simply by shielding the cultivated plants. If deep-rooted perennials are not a problem you can use a contact weedkiller that will act rather like a chemical hoe (a real hoe may be an easier alternative to mixing and applying a weedkiller if the area is small).

3 Once the ground is clear, if you don't want to use a mulch, try applying a weedkiller intended to prevent new weed seedlings emerging. These are only suitable for certain shrubs and fruit crops, but they remain near the surface above root level and only act on seedlings that try to germinate. These should suppress most new weeds for many months.

1 Deep-rooted perennial "problem" weeds, such as bindweed, are best treated by painting on a translocated weedkiller such as one based on glyphosate. Ordinary contact weedkillers may not kill all the roots, but this chemical is moved by the plant to all parts. Even so you may have to treat really difficult weeds a number of times. Use a gel formulation to paint on where watering on the weedkillers may cause damage to adjacent ornamentals.

WEED-FREE PATHS

Paths can easily be kept weed-free for a season using one of the products sold for the purpose. Most of these contain a cocktail of chemicals, some of which act quickly to kill existing weeds and others that prevent the growth of new ones for many months. A single application will keep the path clear for a long time.

Use an improvised shield to prevent the weedkiller being blown onto the flowerbeds.

WORDS OF WARNING

Weedkillers are extremely useful aids, but they can be disastrous if you use the wrong one's, or are careless in their application.

- Always check to see whether it is a total or selective weedkiller.

- If selective, make sure it will kill your problem weeds – and make sure it is suitable for applying to the area you have in mind. Lawn weedkillers should only ever be used on lawns.

- Don't apply liquid weedkillers on a windy day.

- For greater control, use a dribble bar rather than an ordinary rose on your watering-can.

- Keep a special watering-can for weedkillers, otherwise residues may harm your plants.

- Avoid run-off onto flower beds, and if necessary use a shield while applying a weedkiller.

Right: *Paths can be marred by weeds. Either make sure they are mortared between the joints, or use a path weedkiller to keep them looking smart.*

Weed-free Lawns

A weedy lawn will mar your garden, but with modern weedkillers, it's quite easy to eliminate weeds to leave your grass looking like a lawn rather than a mown wild-flower meadow.

KILLING WEEDS IN LAWNS

This method ensures a weed-free lawn with as little as one application a year.

Above: *A lawn like this is the result of regular weeding and feeding. Once weeds have been eliminated, however, the grass should hold its own against new weeds.*

1 Weeds in lawns are best controlled by a selective hormone weedkiller, ideally applied in mid- or late spring. These are usually applied as a liquid, using a dribble bar attached to a watering-can. To ensure even application you should mark out lines with string, spacing them the width of the dribble bar apart.

2 Always mix and apply the weedkiller as recommended by the manufacturer. There are a number of different plant hormones used, some killing certain weeds better than others, so always check that it is recommended for the weeds you most want to control. When mixed, simply walk along each strip slowly enough for the droplets from the dribble bar to cover the area evenly.

3 If your lawn also needs feeding, you can save time by using a combined weed and feed. The most efficient way to apply these – which are likely to be granular rather than liquid – is with a fertilizer spreader.

4 If you have just a few troublesome weeds in a small area, it is a waste of time and money treating the whole lawn. For this job a spot weeder that you dab or wipe onto the offending weed will work well.

Above: *A weed-free lawn leads the eye to a distant patio.*

Right: *The few weeds in this lawn are probably not worth worrying about, but you can easily spot treat an area if you don't want to waste time treating the whole lawn.*

DEALING WITH MOSS

Moss is much more difficult to control than ordinary lawn weeds, and hand weeding is simply not a practical option. Use a moss-killer – some you water on; others are sprinkled on. Ask your garden centre for advice about which is best for your circumstances.

Once the moss has been killed, it is worth trying to avoid the conditions that encourage it: shade and poor drainage.

Feeding

Feeding really does pay dividends. If you see a garden with particularly lush and healthy-looking plants, the chances are they have been well fed.

Feeding used to be a job that had to be tackled several times during the course of a season, and some enthusiasts still feed their plants once a week or even more frequently. If you use modern slow-release and controlled-release fertilizers, however, feeding is something you can do just a couple of times a year.

Liquid feeds, nevertheless, are more instant in effect and still have a use, being invaluable when plants need a quick pick-me-up.

FEEDING CONTAINERS

Container plants require supplementary nutrients to keep them in good health.

■ A controlled- or slow-release fertilizer added to the potting soil at planting time will keep most containers blooming well all summer. Follow the instructions for application rates.

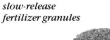
slow-release fertilizer granules

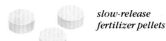
slow-release fertilizer pellets

SLOW- AND CONTROLLED-RELEASE

Some fertilizers are described as slow-release and controlled-release. Both allow the nutrients to seep out into the soil over a period of months, but controlled-release fertilizers are affected by soil temperature. Nutrients are only released when the soil is warm enough for growth in most plants.

slow-release fertilizer sachet

2 If you find it more convenient, you can place sachets of slow-release fertilizer beneath the plants when you plant them.

3 If you can buy pellets of slow-release fertilizer like this, place them beneath individual plants at planting time.

FEEDING THE LAWN

There are several ways to do this, all taking relatively little time.

1 The quickest way to feed your lawn is with a wheeled spreader like this. Although individual models vary, you can usually adjust the delivery rate. Test the rate on a measured area of path first, then sweep up the fertilizer and weigh it to make sure the application rate is right.

2 An easy way to give your lawn a liquid boost is to use a sprinkler system into which you can introduce special fertilizer pellets. It will feed the lawn as it waters, and you don't have to stand there holding the hose.

3 A hose-end dilutor like this is a good way to apply a soluble fertilizer for a quick response. It is much quicker than mixing it in watering-cans to apply. You can use this type of hose-end dilutor for beds and borders as well as for the lawn.

BEDS AND BORDERS

An annual feed will keep even the most demanding plants happy.

1 Most established plants, but especially demanding ones such as roses, benefit from annual feeding. Apply a slow- or controlled-release fertilizer in spring or early summer, sprinkling it around the bushes. Keep it away from the stem, sprinkling it further out where most of the active root growth is.

2 Hoe it into the surface so that it penetrates the root area more quickly.

3 Unless rain is expected, water it in. This will make the fertilizer active more quickly in dry conditions.

soluble fertilizer

INDEX OF COMMON PLANT NAMES

Barberry – *Berberis*
Bay – *Laurus nobilis*
Beech – *Fagus sylvatica*
Begonia, fibrous-rooted – *Begonia semperflorens*
Blazing star – *Liatris*
Bleeding heart – *Dicentra*
Bowles Golden Grass – *Milium effusum 'Aureum'*
Box – *Buxus sempervirens*
Bugle – *Ajuga reptans*
Busy Lizzie – *Impatiens*
Butterfly bush – *Buddleia davidii*
Californian lilac – *Ceanothus*
Chamomile – *Chamaemelum nobile,* syn. *Anthemis nobilis*
Cotton lavender – *Santolina chamaecyparissus*
Cupid's dart – *Catananche caerulea*
Curry plant – *Helichrysum*

italicum
Daffodils – *Narcissus spp*
Day lily – *Hemerocallis*
Elephant ears – *Bergenia*
Feather grass – *Stipa*
Fibrous-rooted begonia – *Begonia semperflorens*
Fishbone cotoneaster – *Cotoneaster horizontalis*
Foam flower – *Tiarella cordifolia*
French marigolds – *Tagetes patula*
Gayfeather – *Liatris*
Geranium, bedding type – *Pelargonium*
Globe thistle – *Echinops*
Hard shield fern – *Dryopteris aculeatum*
Hart's-tongue fern – *Phyllitis scolopendrium,* syn. *Asplenium scolopendrium, Scolopendrium vulgare*
Heather – *Calluna, Erica*

Holly – *Ilex*
Holly fern – *Polystichum falcatum*
Ivy – *Hedera helix*
Jacob's ladder – *Polemonium caeruleum*
Kaffir lily – *Schizostylis coccinea*
Lady's mantle – *Alchemilla mollis*
Lavender – *Lavandula*
Lilac, Californian – *Ceanothus*
Lily – *Lilium*
Lily-of-the-valley – *Convallaria majalis*
Lungwort – *Pulmonaria spp*
Male fern – *Dryopteris filix-mas*
Mallow – *Lavatera*
Marigold, French – *Tagetes patula*
Marigold, pot – *Calendula*
Mexican orange blossom –

Choisya ternata
Michaelmas daisy – *Aster novae-angliae* and *A. novi-belgii*
New Zealand burr – *Acaena*
Parrot feather – *Myriophyllum*
Peony, tree – *Paeonia suffruticosa*
Periwinkle – *Vinca*
Pickerel weed – *Pontederia cordata*
Pink – *Dianthus*
Plantain lily – *Hosta*
Poached egg plant – *Limnanthes douglasii*
Pot marigold – *Calendula*
Red-hot poker – *Kniphofia*
Rock rose – *Helianthemum nummularium*
Rose of Sharon – *Hypericum calycinum*
Rosemary – *Rosmarinus officinalis*

Rue – *Ruta graveolens*
Shuttlecock fern – *Matteuccia struthiopteris*
Silk tassel bush – *Garrya elliptica*
Snow in summer – *Cerastium tomentosum*
Snowdrops – *Galanthus nivalis*
Soft shield fern – *Dryopteris setiferum*
Spotted laurel – *Aucuba japonica* (variegated varieties)
Sweet bay – *Laurus nobilis*
Thrift – *Armeria maritima*
Thyme – *Thymus*
Tree peony – *Paeonia suffruticosa*
Water hawthorn – *Aponogeton distachyus*
Yew – *Taxus baccata*

INDEX

A

Annuals, 42
  self-sowing, 54
Aquatics, planting, 75

B

Bedding plants
  annuals, 42
  perennials, 42
  summer, no-fuss, 43
Beds
  dwarf conifers in, 46, 47
  feeding, 93
  grass, 38, 39
  gravel, 32, 33
  heather, 44, 45
  heathers and conifers, 48, 49
  lawn, in, 20
  mixed, 49
  permanent edge, 42
  seasonal and permanent plants
    in, 42
  shrubs, 30
  weeds in, 88
Black polythene mulches, 85
Borders
  feeding, 93
  grasses in, 39
  herbaceous plants, 30, 34, 35
  mixed, 30, 36
  planting, 34
  shrubs, 30
  tree at back of, 31
  trees in, 52, 53
  weeds in, 88
Bulbs
  established clumps, dividing,
    57
  grass, naturalizing in, 18
  large, naturalizing, 56
  small, naturalizing, 56
Butyl rubber mulches, 85

C

Chamomile lawn, 22
Chemical control, 10
Chemical pruning, 76
Chipped bark mulch, 86, 87
Clay pavers, 26
Climbers
  planting, 78
  self-supporting, 78
  walls and fences, on, 72
Clover lawn, 22
Cocoa shell mulch, 86, 87
Compression sprayer, 10

Conifers
  bed, planting, 46, 47
  containers, in, 64
  dwarf, 46, 47
  ground cover, as, 60
  heathers with, 45, 48, 49
Containers
  automatic watering, 64
  changing pots in, 70
  easy-care, 64, 65
  evergreens, in, 66, 70
  mixed collections in, 66
  perennials in, 68
  replenishment, planting for, 70
  shrubs for, 66
  winter and summer interest, 70
  winter baskets, 71
Cuttings, 22, 61

D

Difficult positions, 61
Dividing plants, 61
Dry soil, plants for, 62
Dwarf conifers, 8, 46, 47

E

Easy plants, 35
Electric trimmers, 76, 77
Evergreens
  containers, in, 66, 70

F

Feeding, 82, 83
  beds and borders, 93
  containers, 92
  controlled release, 93
  lawn, 93
  slow-release, 93
Fences
  climbers on, 72
Fern gardens, 40, 41
Fertilizers, 82
  controlled-release, 93
  slow-release, 93
Flowering shrubs, self-sufficient,
  51
Flowers, self-sowing, 54
Foliage shrubs, self-sufficient, 51
Fruit, 81

G

Garden compost mulch, 86, 87
Garden floor, 16, 17
Grass
  alternatives to, 22, 23
  cutting, 11
  gravel beds in, 32

Grasses
  beds, 38, 39
  borders, in, 39
  planting, 38
Gravel, 16
  weeding, 83
Gravel beds, 32, 33
Gravel gardens, 24
Gravel mulch, 86, 87
Ground cover
  conifers, 60
  heathers, 60
  labour-saving, 58
  non-woody, 58
  planting, 58
  plants for, 8
  raising plants for, 61
  roses, 60
  shrubby, 60
  thyme, 60
  weeds, protection from, 58

H

Hanging basket
  winter, for, 71
Hard landscaping materials, 9
Heathers, 8, 44, 45
  conifers, with, 45, 48, 49
  ground cover, as, 60
  mass planting, 49
Hedges
  area, reducing, 77
  chemical pruning, 76
  cutting, 11
  easy-maintenance, 72
  height reduction, 77
  lifting and replanting, 76
  rate of growth, reducing, 76
  trimmers, 76, 77
Herbaceous border plants, 30, 34,
  35
Hops mulch, 86, 87
Hyacinth bulbs, 18

K

Kitchen garden
  fruit, 80
  potatoes, 80
  sowing aids, 81
  time-saving, 80, 81

L

Lawn, 16
  alternatives to grass, 22, 23
  beds in, 20
  bulbs, naturalizing, 18
  chamomile, 22

clover, 22
  cutting, 11
  cutting width, 21
  feeding, 93
  moss in, 91
  mowing edge, 21
  mowing time, cutting down, 20
  multi-level mowing, 20
  straight edges, 20
  textured effect, 18
  thyme, 22, 23
  tree in, 52
  weeds, killing, 90, 91
  wild-flower, 19
Leaves, raking up, 52
Loose mulches, 84, 86, 87
Low-maintenance gardening
  meaning, 8
  time spent on, 8

M

Manure mulch, 86, 87
Moss, 17
  lawns, in, 91
Mulches, 82
  black polythene, 85
  butyl rubber, 85
  chipped bark, 86, 87
  cocoa shell, 86, 87
  established plants, for, 85
  garden compost, 86, 87
  gravel, 86, 87
  loose, 84, 86, 87
  organic, 82
  peat, 86, 87
  rotted manure, 86, 87
  sawdust, 86, 87
  sheet, 80, 84
  spent hops, 86, 87
  spent mushroom compost, 86,
    87
  wool waste, 85
  woven plastic, 85
Mulching sheet, 80
Mushroom compost mulch, 86, 87

N

Nylon line trimmers, 11

O

Organic mulch, 82

P

Paths, weeding, 89
Patio pool, 75
Paving, 16, 17

clay pavers, 26
  laying, 26, 27
  mix and match materials, 28
  pebble texture, 29
  plants, space for, 28
Peat mulch, 86, 87
Pebble texture, 29
Pebbles, 53
Perennials, 42
  containers, in, 68
  self-sowing, 54
  trough, in, 68
Plastic, planting through, 45
Ponds
  lined, 74
  low-maintenance garden, in, 72
  patio pool, 75
  planting, 75
Pop-up sprinkler, 15
Potatoes
  polythene sheet, grown
    beneath, 80
Pruning
  chemical, 76
  shrubs, 50

R

Reliable plants, 35
Roses
  ground cover, as, 60

S

Sawdust mulch, 86, 87
Seed, raising plants from, 61
Shade, plants for, 62
Sheet mulches, 80, 84
Shrubs
  borders, in, 30
  compact, 50
  containers, in, 66
  flowering, self-sufficient, 51
  foliage, self-sufficient, 51
  planting, 50
  pruning, 50
  self-sufficient, 50, 51
  wall, 78
Sowing aids, 81

T

Thyme
  ground cover, as, 60
  lawn, 22, 23
Tools, labour-saving, 10, 11
Trees
  bare-root, 52
  border, in, 52, 53
  borders, in, 31

INDEX

falling leaves, 52
lawn, in, 52
plants to grow under, 62
Trough
perennials, for, 68

V

Vegetables
low-maintenance garden, in, 72

W

Walls
climbers on, 72, 78
shrubs, 78
Water
lined pools, 74
low-maintenance garden, in, 72
Watering
aids, 14, 15

automatic, 12, 13
containers, 64
drip-feed systems, 12, 14
pop-up sprinkler, 15
Watering-can
dribble bar, 10
Weedkillers, using, 89
Weeds
beds and borders, in, 88

controlling, 88, 89
feeding, 82
ground cover suppressing, 58
lawns, in, 90, 91
mulching sheet, using, 80
paths, in, 89
weedkillers, using, 89
Wild-flower lawn, 19
Wildlife garden, 19

Winter baskets, 71
Wool waste mulches, 85
Woven plastic mulches, 85

ACKNOWLEDGEMENTS

The author and publishers would like to thank the following:

Andy Sturgeon at The Fitted Garden, Garson Farm Garden Centre, Winterdown Road, West End, Esher, Surrey, KT10 8LS, for producing the practical sequences for photography.

Thanks also to Black & Decker, 210 Bath Road, Slough, SL1 3YD and Hazelock Ltd, Haddenham, Aylesbury, Bucks, HP17 8JD for providing the equipment for photography on pages 10 and 11, and thanks to Simon Chapman of Prototype Communications.

PICTURE CREDITS

All special photography by John Freeman. The following photographs © Peter McHoy:

p1, p2 top left and top right, p7, p8 left, p13, p14 top, p17 left, p18 top and bottom right, p19 top, p20 top, p23, p24 bottom left, p25, p30, p31 right, p32 bottom left, p33 right, p35 right, p36 bottom left and top right, p37, p39, p43, p45 top, p49, p51, p53, p55, p57, p59, p60 bottom, p61, p63, p71 right, p73 top and bottom, p74, p76, p77, p78 bottom, p79, p81, p82, p83, p85 top.